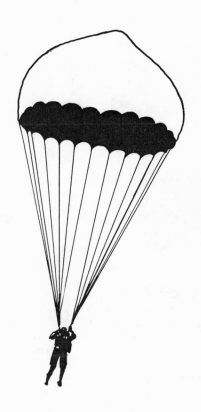

BAT-21

Based on the True Story of
Lieutenant Colonel Iceal E. Hambleton, USAF

William C. Anderson

PRENTICE-HALL, INC., Englewood Cliffs, N.J.

Printed in the United States of America
Prentice-Hall International, Inc., London
Prentice-Hall of Australia, Pty. Ltd., Sydney
Prentice-Hall of Canada, Ltd., Toronto
Prentice-Hall of India Private Ltd., New Delhi
Prentice-Hall of Japan, Inc., Tokyo
Prentice-Hall of Southeast Asia Pte. Ltd., Singapore
Whitehall Books Limited, Wellington, New Zealand

10 9 8 7 6 5 4 3 2 1

Library of Congress Cataloging in Publication Data

Anderson, William C
    BAT-21.

    1. Hambleton, Iceal E.   2. United States. Air
Force—Biography.   3. Air pilots, Military—United
States—Biography.   4. Vietnamese Conflict, 1961-1975
—Biography.   5. Escapes.   I. Title.
UG626.2.H33A64   959.704′348′0924 [B]   80-20648
ISBN 0-13-069500-9

ACKNOWLEDGEMENTS

I am deeply indebted to many people for their assistance in developing this book, especially the following, who made vital contributions to the project:

Lieutenant Colonel C.B. Kelly, Chief of the Los Angeles Office of Information of the Secretary of the Air Force, who first brought the Hambleton story to my attention after its declassification by the Air Force.

Colonel Donald Burggrabe, who carried through with unflagging enthusiasm upon Colonel Kelly's retirement from the Air Force.

Brigadier General H. J. Dalton, Director of Air Force Public Affairs, who shared our enthusiasm for the project and opened many doors.

Donald Baruch, of the Public Affairs Office for the Secretary of Defense, who was instrumental in providing Department of Defense cooperation.

Marjorie Johnson, whose help in researching and drafting the book is deeply appreciated.

I acknowledge the invaluable assistance and cooperation of Lieutenant Colonel Iceal E. Hambleton and his gracious wife, Gwen, without whose help the miraculous story of a true Vietnam hero would never have been told.

William C. Anderson

CONTENTS

First Day   *1*
Second Day   *15*
Third Day   *31*
Fourth Day   *45*
Fifth Day   *63*
Sixth Day   *73*
Seventh Day   *89*
Eighth Day   *103*
Ninth Day   *119*
Tenth Day   *135*
Eleventh Day   *149*
Twelfth Day   *165*
Thirteenth Day   *177*
Author's Afterword   *185*

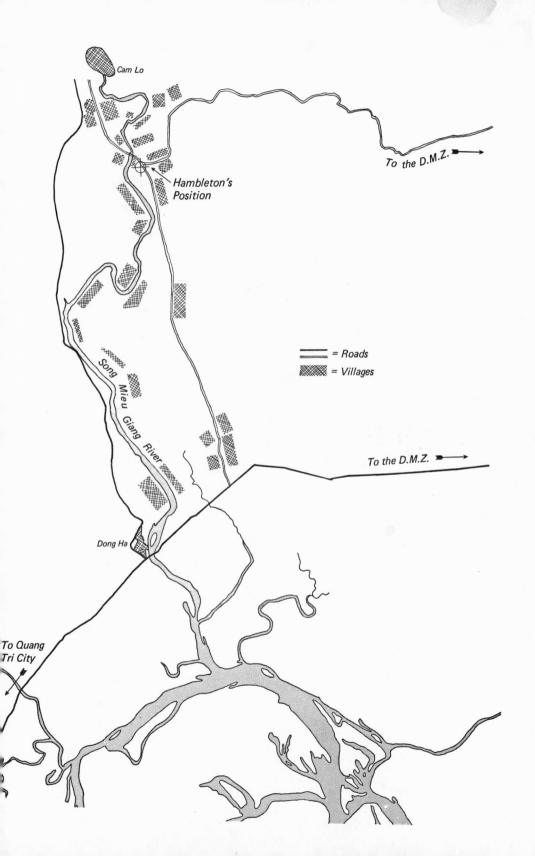

Cam Lo

Hambleton's
Position

To the D.M.Z.

Song Mieu Giang River

= Roads
= Villages

To the D.M.Z.

Dong Ha

To Quang
Tri City

The First Day

The hammer fell on Easter Weekend, 1972. Soon after midnight, in the early-morning darkness of Good Friday, 30 March, thousands of Communist mortar, rocket and artillery rounds began battering South Vietnamese positions along the northern border of the Republic. By mid-day, multitudes of North Vietnamese regulars had moved across the so-called Demilitarized Zone (DMZ), assaulting fire bases and linking with other Communist units already to the south. Bewildered by the mass and ferocity of the attacks ... the defenders quickly fell back from the advanced posts.
—from "Airpower and the 1972 Spring Invasion," United States Air Force

Hambleton squirmed uncomfortably in his seat.

It always amazed him that a big plane like an EB-66 could be so cramped inside. Maybe it was because his six-foot-two frame was never intended to fit into the tight space that made up the navigator's position. But probably, Hambleton thought ruefully, it was just because he was simply too old for this kind of thing. At fifty-three he shouldn't be flying combat, and doubtless wouldn't be if the Air Force hadn't been in need of his special skills right now.

In fact, now more than ever. The new North Vietnamese offensive was only two days old, but already three divisions of enemy troops, strongly supported by Russian-made tanks, had overrun the DMZ and were driving rapidly south toward Quang Tri City. Until—and if—the situation could be stabilized, every Air Force plane and flier in South Vietnam would be needed on the line. Even Hambleton's hopes of taking the brief, long-planned R and R with Gwen were now in ruins. As matters stood, it would probably be quite a while before he and his wife would be able to soak up the sunshine on Bangkok's Don Maun golf course.

But at least the present mission didn't seem too bad. Takeoff had been right on the money and the tanker refueling had gone as smooth as goose grease. The objective—electronically sweeping an area south of Ban Kari Pass just prior to the arrival of a cell of B-52's—would only require the two EB-66's in Hambleton's flight to be over the target for about fifteen minutes. And as long as they stayed south of the former DMZ, they wouldn't have to worry about SAMs. All in all, a piece of cake.

As if reading his mind, the voice of the pilot came into his headset. "Helluva way to spend Easter Sunday. Right, Ham?"

Hambleton thumbed his intercom button. "I'll drink to that."

"Might get back in time to do nine holes. You buy those new clubs you've been ogling at the BX?"

"Had to. Self-defense. Wanted to be ready for Don Maun. Great course. You should play it sometime."

"Not with you. I've lost so much money playing with you I'm listing you as a dependent on my income tax."

Hambleton chuckled. "It's all in how you keep score. I lie a lot."

"How're we doing on our ETA?"

Hambleton checked his navigational log. "Holding good. ETA over station at sixteen-forty. Ten minutes."

"Roger. You crows in back wake up. Crank up your jamming equipment. Wouldn't do for SAC to get their tail feathers ruffled. Stand by to dispense chaff."

A microphone click by one of the electronics officers in the rear of the plane acknowledged the pilot's transmission.

Hambleton addressed himself to his electronic monitoring console. He knew the "crows" in the back of the plane—four electronic warfare officers—were doing the same.

The mission of the old Douglas EB-66 airplane—lovingly called Souieee by its crews (among other names not so loving)—was the highly classified, unsung, and unglamorous job of radar surveillance. This was used in support of nearly every Air Force combat mission. It was the task of an EB-66 crew of six to sweep for enemy radar and jam it, to clear a path for the fighters and bombers that would follow.

Hambleton, seated behind and to the right of the pilot, was

the busiest of all the crew members. He served as copilot, engineer, navigator, and part-time electronics officer. In this latter capacity he now routinely turned on the modes to activate the equipment that would detect the launching of any deadly enemy SAM (Surface to Air Missile) fired from the ground. In the unlikely event that any SAM's were in the area, this information would be invaluable. It provided as much as a ten-second warning, allowing the pilot to whip over into a SAM break—a violent flying maneuver that caused the homing missile to exceed its gimbal limits and destroy itself as it tried to follow the wild gyrations of its target.

With the set warmed up, Hambleton switched to the High Power mode, lit a cigarette, and relaxed. After sixty-three missions it was all boringly routine. For seven months he had been cramming his cranium into a brain-bucket helmet and crawling into an antiquated EB-66 blowtorch like some addled Don Quixote off to joust with the rice paddies. Stupid goddamn war! So hedged in with stupid ground rules and political misgivings there was no hope of winning it. And now, just when Gwen ...

"SAM ON SCOPE!"

The words from the rear of the aircraft smashed into Hambleton's headset, jerking him upright. He scanned his panel. There was no warning light indicating a launch. How in hell could the crows in back paint a missile on scope? As he reached for his mike button to verify, the pilot was already whipping over into a left SAM break. And then, looking down, he saw it. Incredibly, the missile was coming straight up at them!

The rocket struck and exploded with a thunderous impact. Stunned with the realization that the missile had detonated in the rear of the plane where the EWOs were staioned, Hambleton froze in his seat. He was vaguely aware of the pilot's hand reaching for the bail-out button. And then the harsh jangle of the bail-out bell jerked him to his senses. He fumbled for the firing mechanism of his ejection seat, found it, and—following long-rehearsed bail-out procedures—squeezed the trigger. The compressed-air cylinder under him exploded with the jolt of a mule's kick shooting him out of the top of the plane.

And suddenly he was alone in the air, six miles above the alluvial fields of Vietnam.

Spinning through space, Hambleton felt his seat separate from him as the ejection cycle continued. At thirty thousand feet the thin air was numbing cold as it lashed at him, resisting his five-hundred-mile-an-hour velocity. Then his problems compounded: He found himself in a flat spin.

His training had taught him that the centrifugal force of a fast spin could quickly black him out. Normally it would be wise to free-fall through the cold, rarefied atmosphere until his chute popped open automatically at fourteen thousand feet. Down there the environment was much warmer and friendlier. But it had not been a normal ejection; something had gone wrong and sent him spinning out of the aircraft. Should he risk the exposure to cold and anoxia at that high altitude? Or should he try and snap himself out of his spin?

Growing dizzier by the second, he made the decision. He pulled the manual rip cord. The nylon whooshed from his back-pack, billowed out, and popped with a shock. His free-fall was abruptly stopped with a neck-snapping jolt. He hung now at the end of the chute's risers, gently swinging in wide oscillations like the pendulum of a great-grandfather's clock.

Dazed and fighting panic, he looked around. There should be other nylon blossoms popping in the blue sky. He swung around full circle. There were none. Then he spotted the plume of smoke below him, spiraling down like a huge sinister corkscrew. He followed it with his eyes until it disappeared into a low bank of clouds.

He could see no chutes....

A wave of nausea hit him and he went limp in his harness. Five of his old friends. Wiped out within seconds. What the hell had gone wrong? But for the grace of God—and the SAM break that had left him the least vulnerable to the explosion—he would be with them! *Sweet mother of Jesus!*

Completely numbed by the shock, he dangled in his chute, unable to take his eyes from the fading twist of smoke below him. And then as he watched, the plume began to blur. Odd. He looked away. He looked through his swinging feet to the cloud deck far below. It, too, was swimming. So was the horizon. What the hell? Was it shock that completely clouded his vision? And then, the instinct for survival surfacing through his emotion, he realized. Good God! Oxygen! He was in the rarefied atmosphere!

Frantically he fumbled at the side of his chute pack and pulled out the rubber hose attached to the small cylinder of oxygen. He stuck the tube into his mouth, yanked the little "green apple" knob that started the oxygen flowing from the bail-out bottle, and began sucking. He took deep breaths. With overwhelming relief he noticed his vision was clearing. Things were coming back into focus. Careful, Hambone, he told himself, ease up! Too much oxygen could be as dangerous as too little. He inhaled more slowly. He began to feel better, almost giddy as the blue-fingernail signs of anoxia were dispelled by the life-giving oxygen.

Damn, it was quiet up here! It was the first time he had ever had to bail out. Under different circumstances the nylon descent might even have been enjoyable. But there was something wrong with the harness. He reached down to adjust a strap, and as he did so, noticed that the glove on his left hand was dripping blood. More out of curiosity than concern, he peeled off the glove. There was a nasty gash on his index finger. It had undoubtedly happened as he ejected. He had hung up on something. That was what had sent him spinning through space.

He knew it would take some twenty minutes to parachute thirty thousand feet. He might as well put the time to good use. He reached into his survival vest, pulled out his first-aid kit, and proceeded to disinfect the wound and bandage it. Then, as he floated silently under his nylon umbrella, he replaced the kit, donned his glove, and began to assess his situation.

Where in hell was he? He dredged his memory for the last position he had made on his navigational charts. Luckily he had plotted a position shortly before the missile hit. Mentally calibrating the elapsed time, he figured he was over the Cam-Lo area. Maybe a dozen miles south of the DMZ.

The Demilitarized Zone! His hazy memory of the premission briefing kicked out a disquieting thought. Depending on how far south the invading forces had come during the night, he could be floating down into the midst of forty thousand enemy troops in the big push toward Quang Tri. Christ on a crutch!

Time to deactivate his beeper. He reached around his parachute harness for the little built-in radio that automatically started sending out a signal when the canopy was popped. Its purpose was to send out a homer for aircraft searching for him when he was down, but it could just as easily lead unfriendly troops to his position. He pushed the button to silence it.

He instinctively pulled up his feet as he entered a thick cloud layer. The temperature was getting warmer. He had to start thinking about landing. Floating through the milky mist, he broke out between cloud layers. As he did so he saw something that brought him up short.

It was an 0-2! A little American puddle-jumper airplane used by forward air controllers to direct fighters and artillery to enemy objectives. To his amazement he saw he was descending right through the center of the small plane's orbit.

At first glance he was overjoyed at seeing an American airplane. A friendly. But then a sobering thought hit him: The little FAC 0-2's were used in very close support to pinpoint enemy targets. The presence of the plane here could only mean one thing. He must be coming down very near enemy troops. In fact, he could be landing right in the middle of them.

He reached into his vest and pulled out the small survival radio. He switched it on and began calling. "Oh-two. FAC Oh-two. Come in."

To his surprise the response was immediate. "This is FAC Oh-two, call sign Birddog. Identify yourself."

"This is Bat Twenty-one." Hambleton used the call letters of his aircraft. "Bat Twenty-one. Look up, Birddog. I'm the parachute at about twelve grand. Coming down in the middle of your orbit."

There was a pause, then, "Son of a bitch!"

"I think I need help," Hambleton transmitted. Then he felt a little foolish. Hanging up there like a puppet on a string, that last transmission might be termed superfluous.

"Bat Twenty-one. Homed in on your beeper. Have you in sight. Can the chatter. Gooks monitor this frequency. Will advise. Happy landings."

"Roger." Hambleton clicked off. Time to get ready for landing. He sure as hell hoped it would be happy. He looked below him. With relief he saw that fingers of coastal fog had groped in from the sea, covering the low-lying terrain beneath him with a thick blanket. At least he wouldn't be visible for target practice as he swung helplessly under his canopy.

Closer to the ground he started picking up the sound of heavy mortars and the popping of small-arms fire. Beautiful! Nothing like making your first emergency parachute drop into the middle of a firefight!

As he entered the layer of ground fog, he got into impact

position. Dimly, he sensed rather than saw the ground leaping up to meet him. Then he hit hard and tumbled, unhooking his chute harness as he rolled. Disentangling himself, he looked quickly around him. He was in the center of a dry rice paddy. The thump of mortars and the noise of big guns seemed to circle him.

Had he been observed? He wasted no time finding out. In the center of the rice paddy he felt as naked as a lone eight ball on a billiard table. Crouching low, he sprinted to the first cover he spotted, a low ditch that rimmed the rice field. He flung himself into it, lying prostrate while he caught his breath.

The firing continued, but apparently it wasn't aimed at him. At least not yet. He took a moment for personal inventory. All his limbs seemed to respond normally. He checked the gash on his finger. It had stopped bleeding. He seemed to be in one piece. He ran his hand over his face and discovered a startling thing. He was wearing his Air Force reading glasses! Half prescription, half plain glass, he rarely used them except for close work—which is why he had had them on when he ejected; he had been using them to work on his navigational charts. Miraculously, the glasses had stayed firmly on his nose all through punch-out, descent, and landing.

He was suddenly hit by the incongruity of the situation. Here he was, hunkered down in a ditch in the middle of a combat zone, wearing these ridiculous reading glasses. Well, by God, if they had stuck with him this long—if *they* had survived—he damned well could too. He decided he'd leave them on. By wearing them, there was less chance of their getting broken than if he carried them in a pocket of his flight suit. Anyway, there was something homey about them. They made him think of Gwen. And Pierre. Now if he only had his pipe and slippers ...

Something caught his eye.

It was his parachute! Lying in the far corner of the rice paddy, it was barely visible in the swirling fog.

A dead giveaway! Even though his descent had been masked by ground fog, he knew the enemy would be looking for him. If the Birddog pilot had homed in on his parachute beeper before he had clicked it off, chances are the gomers had too. And the radio transmission—even brief—would be a giveaway, using Guard channel. With the going price of a lieutenant colonel's head in the Vietcong marketplace, they'd leave no stone unturned to find him. Even in the middle of a big offensive.

There was no alternative. He'd have to dash from cover to retrieve his telltale chute. As he gathered himself for the sprint, the *harrrumph* of a bursting mortar shell in the middle of the field changed his mind. Rather than risk life and limb trying to bury the chute, it might be prudent to let it stay right where it was. Besides, it wouldn't be long before the Jolly Greens arrived to pick him up.

He settled himself into the ditch, making himself as comfortable as possible. Fighting to control his breathing and his pounding heart, he waited for the first sound of chopper rotors.

His flares were at the ready, to mark the spot.

The revving of the Birddog's two little push-me-pull-you engines overhead suddenly snapped Hambleton to attention. He switched on his radio. "Bat Twenty-one," came the pilot's voice. "This is Birddog. QSY to Baker channel."

"Roger." Hambleton channeled his radio. "Birddog, Bat Twenty-one. How do you read on Baker?"

"Five square, Bat. Everybody and his dog uses Guard channel. May take the gooks a while to pick up this frequency. How you doin'?"

"Good shape."

"Outstanding. What's your dog's name?"

Hambleton blinked at his radio. His dog's name? Then he remembered. Like every American flier assigned to Asia, he had had to fill out a secret card for his personal folder listing four questions and the answers, which only he knew. This was to provide positive identification in the event he were ever shot down in combat. After much head scratching he had filled out his card and sealed it in the secret envelope, to be opened only if he were downed behind enemy lines:

Question	Answer
1. What's your favorite color?	Red
2. Who's your favorite athlete?	Ernie Banks (shortstop for Chicago Cubs)
3. What's your dog's name?	Pierre (French poodle)
4. What's your favorite hobby?	Golf

He had thought it all pretty silly at the time. And now, Jesus! Here he was, shot down in enemy territory and actually being queried from his secret card. It had all happened so fast! For the first time the gravity of his situation hit him.

"Dog's name's Pierre," he managed.

"Spell it. Phonetically."

"Peter Item Easy Roger Roger Easy."

There was a pause before Birddog responded. "You *are* an old-timer. Would you believe Papa India Echo Romeo Romeo Echo?"

Damn! In his confusion he had resorted to the old, outdated phonetic alphabet. At a time like this! "Roger, Birddog."

"Who's your favorite sports player?"

"Ernie Banks."

Another short pause, then, "Positive identification, Bat Twenty-one. We'll get you out. But not tonight. Weather stinks. Dig in. Pick you up in the morning."

Hambleton tried to acknowledge with a cheery reply that aborted in his throat as he clicked off. *The morning!* Would he still be a free man in the morning? Would he even be alive?

If he were stuck for the night he had to find a safer place. As far as possible from that parachute. He peered over the edge of the ditch and dimly made out a wooded area to the west. If he could make it to the protection of those trees....

He memorized the terrain as best he could through the scudding fog and took a compass line on a likely looking spot to dig in. It seemed his best chance for safe cover during the night.

Then he lay back, stretched out and tried his damndest to look like a ditch as he nervously waited for darkness to fall.

The night settled down around Hambleton like a black, damp shroud. There were only the rays of a tyro moon trying to filter through scraps of fog that lined the low pockets of terrain. It ought to be dark enough to seek safer surroundings.

He sat up and looked around, listening. Things seemed fairly quiet. He crawled stealthily out of the ditch, crouching low and moving swiftly toward the line of trees. Reaching it, he darted along a thick hedge lined with dense undergrowth until he found his memorized spot.

He dove into the foliage and lay still, listening to the heart thumping in his chest. Had anyone seen him? Followed him? He lay still for a long time, trying to quiet his heavy breathing. All seemed to be serene. Maybe the fog was holding up the war.

Cautiously he moved to a sitting position. His eyes had adjusted to the darkness, and peeking out of the foliage he could see no signs of life. Good show. Except for the remote boom of heavy guns, there was no noise.

After an hour of alert apprehension, a sort of languor crept over him. He seemed to be safe for the moment. And farther away from that damned parachute he felt more secure. It was time to get his life in some kind of order. He would start with a personal inventory.

Methodically he went through the pockets of his flying suit. For combat flying it had been stripped of its name tag, usually worn over the left pocket, but there were lieutenant colonel's silver leaves sewn on the shoulders. Would he be smart to cut them off? In case of capture. ... To hell with it! He wasn't going to get captured. The Jolly Greens would be picking him up in the morning.

His flight-suit pockets produced very little. In his hasty departure from the airplane he had left his cigarettes, matches, and gum. What he wouldn't give for that half of a Mounds candy bar he had left on the navigator's console! And a cigarette. God, he craved a smoke! All he had salvaged were his damned reading glasses, which he needed like a turtle needed an afterburner. And his flying helmet, for which there didn't seem to be any obvious need down here in the mud.

He turned to his survival vest. A search through it proved much more productive than the one through the pockets of his flying suit. The survival vest was just that: a vest that zipped up the front and was worn over the flying suit, containing an astonishing array of survival gear. It was issued to all flying personnel—a mandatory item to be worn on combat missions. It had a lot of pockets, which Hambleton explored one at a time, dumping their contents into his lap.

When he finished he found his inventory contained the following: the first-aid kit; survival radio with extra batteries; tourniquet, which he hoped to God he wouldn't need; flares for helping the rescue choppers spot him; folding plastic water bag— empty; hunting knife; signal mirror; strobe light with infra-red capacity; .38 revolver with 20 rounds of ammo; mosquito netting; a compactly folded 2-foot-square rubber map of the country; a compass small enough to be shoved up his rectum in the event of capture; and insect repellant.

Looking at all this heaped in his lap, Hambleton felt a strange sense of security. A hint of a grin touched the corners of his mouth as he loaded the .38 and crammed the other articles back into their pockets. Survival gear, he thought to himself. Issued for survival. And this is one old poop who's by God going to survive! This stuff might not outfit a bachelor's pad, but it might come in damned handy in a foxhole. Speaking of which...

Locating a spot surrounded by the tallest thickets, he unsheathed his knife and started digging in the soft dirt. It took over an hour to scoop out enough earth to accommodate his tall frame. He spread the dirt out over a large area, covered it with leaves, and did his best in the dark to make it look like the natural surroundings. Then he raked up a pile of leaves and branches, put them near the hole, crawled in, and covered himself with the shrubbery. Pillowing his head on his flying helmet, he snuggled down.

All in all, things could be worse. Much worse. Except for his finger, he had arrived in pretty good shape. He had gone to at least three survival schools during his military career to prepare him for just such an emergency. Now would be a good time to put that learning to the test.

All his instructors had preached fundamentally the same sermon—the old bromide that the main thing to fear was fear itself. Rule out fear and, too, rule out panic. Panic had claimed more victims trying to survive than had malnutrition. Men had survived the most harrowing situations by keeping their heads. OK, he would too.

Not that it would be all roses. He had been taught he would have to use undergrowth, holes, burrows; the same habitat that wild predators used to escape detection. He would obviously have to be wary of the enemy. But there would also be snakes and poisonous insects and other neighbors whose territorial imperative he would be invading. Still, he could do it if he mastered panic.

The survival schools had maintained that the worst thing about bailing out into a foreign, unfriendly environment was the uncertainty, fear of the unknown. Brave men, oddly enough, were sometimes less adaptable to adverse survival conditions than those less brave. The idea was that the gutsy ones were used to being in command of a situation; when they were thrust out of this position they had trouble coping. The nonheroes often adapted more easily to strange circumstances. Hambleton hadn't completely bought this philosophy, but if it were true it was another point in his favor. He thought of himself as anything but a hero. Grandstand plays weren't his style. He'd rather run interference—one reason he was a navigator instead of a pilot. He was a man of common clay, so to speak, and quite content with his modest role in life.

The school solution for long-term survival was to take one step at a time. Accomplish some task each day, no matter how trivial. *Something* that would show progress, provide a feeling of accomplishment, climb one more rung on the ladder to rescue.

Hambleton sighed. Of course all this was academic, and it wouldn't apply to him. He would be rescued tomorrow. The Jolly Greens would probably be coming in at daybreak. But it didn't hurt to review the finer techniques of the art of survival. Besides, thinking about it took his mind off his throbbing finger.

Another thing he had been taught was to be very careful not to overemphasize the negative. Was he guilty of this? Maybe he was being too concerned about the enemy. He hadn't actually *seen* any of them. It was entirely possible the Communists had not picked up his parachute beeper or the short radio transmission on Guard channel. Thanks to the ground fog, his landing could have gone undetected. And even if his chute had been found, it could just as easily have been found by a villager more interested in profit than in the Communist party. At a local flea market, the expensive nylon could be used for barter.

Then there was the fact that he had only a rough idea where he had landed. Maybe he was in an area the enemy's southbound push had not yet reached. Indeed, the mortar and small-arms fire he had heard could have come from the *South* Vietnamese. Maybe he wasn't even in enemy territory. Hell, maybe there wasn't even anybody looking for him.

Pursuing this rationale, his spirits rose. At any rate, he was alive. And so far, free. Which was a hell of a lot better than having his head on a pike in some Communist camp. Or maybe worse, being on his way to the Hanoi Hilton. Or, merciful God, being one of his crewmates who had gone to fiery deaths hours before.

Cool it! Forget it! He had to think good things. Think happy. Think about Gwen. Think about how you're going to love her like she has never been loved in her life. Think about the beautiful new golf course in Bangkok that—

He slapped his cheek. Whatever had been crawling on it splattered unpleasantly. He reached into his vest for his insect repellant and applied it to his exposed areas. Then he leaned back in his hole and again tried to relax.

But now his stomach was growling. It was hungry! *He* was hungry! And thirsty as hell! A ridiculous thought popped into his head. This is Sunday night. Twofer night at the officer's club. Two Manhattans for the price of one. And to celebrate this Easter Sunday there would be a steak cookout at the club. He checked his watch. Going on right now.

He sighed. He always splurged on Sunday dinner. Steak, mushrooms, big baked potato with sour cream and chives—the works. Chased by a liter of red Thai wine. Sometimes followed by a cigar. At least a cigarette. God, he craved a cigarette!

He ran his tongue over his lips and grimaced at the taste of the insect repellant.

It occurred to him that he had no higher priority than getting some sleep, for he had to be fully alert for the pickup in the morning. He would resort to a soporific of his own invention that had never failed him before. He would compose a formal and intensely boring military letter. Usually he was asleep before he even got past the salutation.

But sleep was slower than usual in coming. He was well into the explanation to the Air Force Inspector General about how frustrating it was to try and survive with unbrushed, furry teeth, before drowsiness began to overtake him. He was almost to the recommendation that a toothbrush be included in every survival vest when he finally succumbed to an uneasy, jerking slumber.

The Second Day

It was a strange noise in the early dawn that brought Hambleton struggling up out of his fitful sleep. It was a different sound from the sporadic din of the war around him.

It was the grumble of heavy machinery.

He opened his eyes and looked cautiously out of his hole. Nothing was stirring within the periphery of his vision save an odd-looking bird fighting a decisive battle with a worm. Remnants of the night fog were being dissipated by the rays of the early morning sun. Here, at least, the world seemed at peace, almost idyllic. He could almost have been camping by one of his favorite fishing streams in Arizona.

He wiggled his toes, clenched his fists, forced circulation into cramped limbs. Surely in the protection of the patchy mist he could risk investigating the source of that noise. For as he listened, he was beginning to recognize the sound of trucks among the throaty diesel roar of heavy machinery. Probably military equipment. Were they friendly? If so his problems were over. And if they were unfriendly he had to notify Birddog. Either way he had to investigate.

Cautiously he climbed out of his hole. He stretched on all fours like a hunting dog, then—realizing he might have to find his hole again quickly—he oriented himself. Not far from his nest was a fairly large tree with a distinctively gnarled trunk. He made a mental note of it, then started off, furtively creeping through the undergrowth in the direction of the noise. Slowing as he neared the perimeter of his grove, he sank down on his stomach and squirmed until he came to the last of the hedgerow. He parted the foilage. What he saw made him draw in his breath.

In front of him was a broad highway humming with military vehicles of every description. He didn't need to see their markings to know this rolling stock hadn't been manufactured in Detroit. It was mostly Russian equipment, bearing the strange hieroglyphics of the North Vietnamese Army. And all of it was heading south.

His eyes followed the road as it swung in from the left. There was another road coming down from the north, joining the east-west road at a busy intersection. Then he realized where he was. He remembered it instantly from his navigational charts. He was close, much too close, to the major intersection where Highway 561 came down from the north to intersect 8B, running east and west. This would be a major branch-off route for the Communist armies heading south. He had managed to bail out directly over one of the busiest intersections of the Communist supply routes!

As if watching a military review, he studied the paraphernalia parading by in front of him: camouflaged tanks, trucks, heavy guns, truckloads of troops—the growling sinews of mechanized war. As they thundered by, churning a cloud of dust that mixed with the ground fog, a group of soldiers standing at the side of the road caught Hambleton's attention. Curious, he watched them, almost amused by their animated gesticulations.

And then he was no longer amused. Some of the gesticulation had evolved into finger pointing—at times in his direction. Suddenly, as if in response to a command, the group split up and started fanning out, leaving one soldier standing by the side of the road. Abruptly Hambleton's bemused curiosity changed to acute shock.

The soldier left behind was standing beside a small mountain of nylon.

It was his parachute!

Hambleton groaned inwardly. There was no longer any doubt about which side of the lines he had chuted into. Nor was there any question as to whether his bail-out had been detected. The enemy must know the general area in which he was hiding. Now there would be an all-out, intensive effort to find him.

Hambleton squirmed back into the protection of the undergrowth, and crouching low, sprinted back toward his hideout. He spotted the tree with the gnarled trunk and quickly homed in on his hole. Flopping into it, he fumbled for his radio and clicked it on. "Birddog from Bat Twenty-one," he whispered breathlessly.

"Come in, Bat Twenty-one."

Thank God Birddog was already in the air. "Patrols. Coming this way."

"Roger, Bat. We'll drop some gravel. Blink your mirror."

"Wilco. Stand by." Hambleton searched through the pockets of his survival vest until he unearthed the small rectangular mirror with the hole in the center. Searching the sky, he spotted the little plane circling high above him and to the south. He took a bead on the plane through the hole in the mirror, and flashed the reflection of the low-slung sun at the high-flying airplane three times.

Presently, "Roger, Bat Twenty-one. Position marked. Birddog out."

Hambleton hoped to hell no one else had seen the flickering mirror that marked his position. He covered the mirrored surface with the palm of his hand to shield any flash and replaced it in his vest. Nothing to do now but wait.

And pray a lot.

He didn't have long to wait. Within minutes came the drone of a flight of A-1E airplanes. Called Sandy, the Douglas A-1E was the oldest combat airplane in the Air Force's inventory. Prop driven (and, in most configurations, a single seater), it had been the Navy's standard dive-bomber in the years following World War II. Miraculously, it was still proving its worth a quarter of a century later in the jet-age combat of Vietnam. Now manned mainly by pilots of the Search and Air-Rescue teams, this long-range, highly maneuverable plane was often employed in providing cover for downed airmen. For an antique it carried a potent sting.

The Sandy pilots roared in, noisy as hell. Their arrival was not supposed to be a secret. If the enemy knew an area was seeded with gravel they avoided it like the plague. And rightly so. Gravel was a little Marquis de Sade touch introduced in the Vietnam War.

A tiny, innocent-looking explosive about the size of a lemon, it was a mine released in large numbers from low-flying aircraft. Dropped in a frozen state, it hit the ground and, upon thawing, armed itself and sent out a web of feelers in all directions, like the tentacles of an octopus. Brushing one of the feelers might not prove fatal, but the explosion could neatly separate a person from an arm or leg. Further refinements to the tiny mine sometimes included its camouflage in the form of dog feces, a form employed with considerable success in keeping invaders off the Ho Chi Minh trail.

On the first pass he heard the rattle of the little mines dumping nearby. Immediately the sound of small-arms fire opened up around him. Completely ignoring the fusillade, the feisty A-1E's darted low, making pass after pass. The drops were done with precision and thoroughness. Not until he was encircled by a ring of gravel beginning some distance from his hole did the pilots make their last shrieking pass and head for home.

With the departure of the Sandys the hellish racket was replaced by an eerie silence. Hambleton could distinguish the high-pitched, excited voices of the Vietnamese rising above the growl of the war machinery, but they were in the distance. He was now protected by a ring of explosives. He felt a little more easy. Only one small problem: The landmines were keeping the enemy out, but they also restricted his own movements to an area perhaps a little more than one square mile. This definitely could have drawbacks, especially when the Jolly Greens arrived.

But on the positive side, his buddies knew exactly where he was holed up. They knew exactly what they were doing and there were a lot of them on high looking out for him. Somewhat comforted by this thought, he again took stock of his situation.

He could see patches of low-lying fog still clinging to the terrain. It would be a while before they burned off, allowing the Jolly Greens to come in low with clear visibility. Best he just stay put for the time being. Just dig in and make as little movement as possible in case some searchers had gotten inside his barrier before the mine seeding had been completed. He'd just lie cool and look like forest.

He crawled into his hole. He unholstered his gun and made sure it was handy. Then he removed his flight helmet in case it might be spotted, and stuck it into the hole. He hadn't gone through survival-training schools for nothing. He was subscribing precisely to the tenets espoused.

His thoughts roamed to his most impressive instructor back at the school in Clark Air Force Base in the Philippines, trying to recapture all he had said.

The gnarled, tough Air Force sergeant had crushed the skull of a live rattlesnake with his teeth, and skinned it as it quivered.

Then he'd said, "Always remember. If you're ever shot down in Nam you got two strikes against you when you try to hide. Round eyes and white skin. You're gonna stand out like a piss hole in the snow. So the first thing you wanna do is put on the black mosquito netting that's in your survival vest. It'll cover up your white features and it'll keep out mosquitoes and other insects. And in the boondocks of Nam they got insects you wouldn't believe."

Hambleton shuddered inwardly as he recalled the conclusion of the lecture. After demonstrating how to clean the snake, the sergeant had diced it up in small pieces and passed the tidbits around to the class. "Lotsa protein in snake," he had said. "And most snakes are edible. Just don't get bit going after a poisonous one. You may not be able to build a fire if you're in hiding, but even raw they taste pretty good. Like chicken." Hambleton had never been particularly attracted to the idea of eating raw chicken, and hated snakes. He had politely refused the offering. He was now hungry, but he was going to have to get a hell of a lot hungrier before going off in search of snakes.

He reached into his vest and pulled out the mosquito netting. Careful not to tear it, he pulled the hood over his head and drew the net gauntlets up over the sleeves of his flying suit. Then he settled back into his hole and piled leaves up over him. Son of a gun. If Gwen could only see him now.

Gwen. He thought of his pretty wife. And how great it would have been to see her again. He had had reservations at the Erewan, the fabulous old luxury hotel with the old-world charm and new-world plumbing. He had intended to blow his flight pay on the great Bangkok restaurants, to go dancing, to make love, to play golf. His mind went back to the last time they had played golf together. Just the two of them at the Tucson National Golf Course. And he thought of the time they had played at the Air Force base in Turkey when he had shot a hole in one. Swept away by the magic of the moment, he had picked Gwen up and swung her round and round, both of them laughing like loons....

Gwen Hambleton had never been in better spirits. She hummed to herself as she flew around in the living room of her comfortable Tucson home, dusting and tidying up after the morning coffee klatch with the girls. She still had a lot to do to get ready for her trip. But being a well-organized Air Force wife, she had prepared a checklist of all the things that had to be done, and as she did each chore she checked it off.

Let's see. Newspaper canceled; milk canceled; post office notified to hold the mail; night timer on the lamp set; ice maker turned off; arrangements made with the neighbors next door to water the plants; picked up traveler's checks at the bank, and passport and shot records from the safe-deposit box; arrangements made at the kennel for Pierre. Now if she only had her airline tickets...

As if on cue the doorbell rang. Gwen answered it, throwing open the door to admit a breathless young brunette. "Sylvia. Great timing! I had just come to you on my checklist."

"Sorry I'm late, Gwen. You know our Fly-the-Coop Travel Agency. I consider it a success if we get tickets to travelers before their plane leaves. But here's yours, finally."

She handed Gwen an airline ticket folder, then a thick Manila envelope, adding "And here's a bunch of stuff I scraped together on tours and things over there. Now don't forget to see the royal barges. And the Buddha temples. And be sure to eat at that fancy restaurant where they serve curry heartburn and the girls dance with candles in their fingernails."

"Thanks, Sylvia. I'll try and work it all in."

"How I envy you! Here I am in the travel agency business and I haven't even been to Disneyland."

They talked a while, then Sylvia decided she better get on her way. "Good-bye, Gwen. Have a marvelous time. You deserve it. And give old handsome Hambone a great big kiss for me. Tell him to come back home where he belongs."

"That I promise. And thanks again, Sylvia."

As Sylvia's little Mustang disappeared round a corner, Gwen turned to go back in. Then her attention was caught by another car coming down the street. It was a blue staff car. The markings indicated it was from nearby Davis-Monthan Air Base.

Curious, she watched, her hand on the knob of the screen door, wondering where it was headed. Then as it approached her house and crunched to a stop, the curiosity was tinged by an indefinable sense of dread. Unable to move, she leaned against the screen door and watched several solemn people get out of the car and approach her. There was Marge Wilson, her closest friend;

then a nurse; and... "Oh Lord, not that," she thought, the airline tickets wadded in her hand. The base chaplain was with them.

Hambleton stared cross-eyed at a caterpillar inching across the mosquito netting in front of his nose. He had never seen a caterpillar from the underside before, and it fascinated him. Amazing the way the little feet grabbed hold as the multicolored worm undulated across the netting, getting a good purchase with the front feet, drawing the rear feet up as it humped, then repeating the process.

An absurd thought crossed Hambleton's mind. He and this fuzzy little worm had something in common. Hambleton, too, was a caterpillar, eligible to belong to the Caterpillar Club. Now that he had punched out of an airplane he would be invited to join the exclusive organization whose membership consisted of fliers who had been saved by a parachute jump. The club had been so named because the first parachutes were made of silk, which was made by caterpillars. Maybe this little silk spinner would bring him good luck. He suddenly felt a strange sense of kinship with the little insect. He was definitely going to keep protective watch on his fraternity brother.

Must be worse things than being a caterpillar. They don't have to pay taxes. They don't have to worry about their golf swing. And when they get bored all they have to do is push a button and they turn into a butterfly and buzz off. Not a bad deal.

He wished to hell *he* could push a button and fly away.

Speaking of which, where were the Jolly Greens? He raised up to look over the foliage at the countryside around him. The ground fog was all but burned off. They should be coming along any minute. He got his flares out and mentally practiced lighting them. He was ready.

He lay back, listening to the steady drone of the heavy machinery pounding down the highway. Suddenly he jerked upright. Good God! *He hadn't reported that to Birddog!* He had been so concerned with getting gravel dropped to save his own skin that he had completely ignored the intelligence report. Sure, there was a good chance that the Air Force had already taken reconnaissance photos of the area and was even now briefing crews on the targets of opportunity.

But what if they hadn't? Much of the traveling was probably done at night or under the fog cover, and the equipment was heavily camouflaged. A pang of fear slammed him. Those big guns being pulled south were antiaircraft guns! Big-bore and sophisticated, probably 85- or 100-mm. The enemy had undoubtedly set some up to guard the highway intersection—a vital supply lifeline. Maybe they were just waiting for the first Jolly Green to hover into their sights...

Jesus Christ! He was a fool! A selfish, self-centered fool! Sitting around in a foxhole on his dead ass feeling sorry for himself. He just might be the bait in a lethal trap being set for the Jolly Greens. Goddamnit, he was supposed to be a professional soldier! He had to get off his butt and warn them.

He pulled out his radio, switched it on, and whispered into it. "Birddog from Bat Twenty-one."

The response was instantaneous. "Come in Bat Twenty-one. Birddog here."

"Nearby intersection. Where Hollywood Freeway joins the Santa Monica Freeway. Like Friday night rush hour. Many drunks on the highway. Very dangerous. Advise Jolly Greens."

There was a pause then, "Roger, Bat. Your report confirms big eye in the sky. Sending in the black and whites in five minutes."

Hambleton breathed a sigh of relief. So the Air Force reconnaissance photos *had* picked up the mass movement. And now they were sending in Sandys to pave the way for the Jolly Greens. "Roger, Birddog. I'll help you direct traffic."

"Understand, Bat. But keep your tail down."

Hambleton almost laughed. In a few minutes his presence would be the least of the enemy's concern. He crawled out of his hole and started furtively through the undergrowth. In a matter of minutes he had reached a little knoll, the highest ground in the confines of his sanctuary. From here, lying on his belly, he had a clear view of the intersection.

Peeking from his grandstand seat he pulled out his map and watched intently, studying the bumper-to-bumper traffic coming down from the north. When they hit the east-west highway the vehicles fanned out in both directions. There was no doubt this intersection was one of the major staging areas of the big Communist push.

He heard the drone of the FAC airplane coming in low. Small-arms fire from the ground began banging as the little Birddog came in on a zigzag course at treetop level. As it passed overhead Hambleton saw the tail cones of two small rockets belch from under its wings as the 0-2 pulled up, grabbing altitude. The two missiles exploded smack in the center of the highways' intersection, sending a bloom of white smoke blossoming over the converging traffic.

Birddog had marked the target precisely.

Hambleton turned on his radio, adjusting the volume down to a whisper so he could monitor the conversation going upstairs. Since search and air-rescue (SAR) pilots tended speak a jargon all their own, he supposed some of it would be unintelligible to him, but it would at least give him a clue as to how the attack was progressing.

"Birddog to all pilots. I've just marked the target. Come in, Gumshoe."

"Roger," replied a low-pitched voice. "We're overhead your position for pylon turn in forty seconds. We have five hundred GPs retarded and twenty mike mike."

"Roger, Gumshoe," said Birddog. "Do you have the target in sight?"

"Affirmative."

"Clobber that area. Be on alert for explosives and secondaries. Maybe ammo trucks. Remember, we've got a friendly down there. He'd probably appreciate it if you didn't blow up his foxhole. Pinpoint your targets."

"Always do, Birddog. Area clear?"

"The ante's right. Put something in the pot."

"Coming down in trail formation. We'll scramble our eggs first."

"Kindly keep an eye out for your friendly FAC. I'm orbiting four thousand feet to the south."

"Roger. Have you in sight. We'll try not to pluck any tail feathers."

"Outstanding. Birddog out."

The first Sandy came in on the deck so low its black shadow snapped at its heels. It roared toward the target, released its bombs, then whipped up into a sweeping climb as the delayed-action ordnance exploded, sending visible shock waves undulating over the terrain. Plane after plane came roaring down in single file, each sowing its seeds of destruction. Hambleton watched with pride the precision flying of the pilots.

And of the planes. Depickled from last war's storage—the

Cosmoline scraped from her engines and the cocoon plastic from her epidermis—the reliable old Sandy was a Vietnam legend. Her relatively slow speed staying power, and prop-whining maneuverability gave her an edge on her new, mach-busting sisters in ground-attack roles, and she was earning her spurs in yet another war.

A secondary explosion triggered by one of the bombed supply trucks sent a towering pillar of smoke into the sky. "Bingo!" chortled Hambleton aloud. "You guys win the fur-lined gaboon."

"Birddog from Gumshoe," came the low voice of the Skyraider leader. "Heads up. Coming in with a strafe."

"Earn your flight pay," came back Birddog.

Once again the planes streaked in, propellers screaming, smoke streaming from their wings as they fired their 20-mm cannons into the war machinery that glutted the highway. For five minutes the attack was pressed. Then the Skyraider leader checked out with Birddog. "Hello, Birddog from Gumshoe. We're Winchester. Want us to reload and come back?"

"Gumshoe from Birddog. Reload and stand by at base. The sports cars are coming in now."

"Wilco."

"Nice shootin', Gumshoe. I'm buying the drinks."

"I heard that, Birddog. Gumshoe out."

As Hambleton observed the attack he had noticed several antiaircraft batteries opening up around him. He had been right. The intersection was ringed with ack-ack. Hambleton had actually felt the ground tremble from the recoil of some heavier-caliber weapons as they tried to shoot down the feinting Sandys that zoomed in at rice-paddy level to foil the radar and computers.

The first batteries firing nearby had scared the devil out of him. He had mistaken the booming of the heavy guns for incoming bombs, and couldn't figure out why the friendlies were bombing so close. Then he had observed the flashes of the guns. The ack-ack shells exploding overhead rained down tiny pieces of pot metal like buckshot, and he was glad he had worn his helmet.

Each time he saw either one of the large guns or multiple implacements of automatic weapons fire, he made a mental note of their camouflaged positions and spotted them on his survival map. Then he called Birddog.

"Birddog, Bat Twenty-one. Ack-ack guns on hill thirty-one."

"Roger, Bat. Stand by," said Birddog.

"Birddog from Crabtree, over," said a voice twanging with a Texas accent.

"Roger, Crabtree. Birddog here."

"We're on station at nineteen grand. We have eight seven-hundred-fiftys and six five-hundred-pound snake eyes and twenty mike mike."

"Roger, Crabtree. Primary target fairly well clobbered. Ack-ack guns reported on hill thirty-one. See if you can pull their plug. Come in when ready."

"Roger, Birddog," came the voice that sounded like a guitar twang. "Comin' in."

It was the first time Hambleton had seen Phantoms in action close up. He had bent elbows with some of the F-4 pilots at the bar: blowtorch jockeys who generally wore white scarves and cowboy boots and who all seemed to hail from Texas. They tended to be a bit tiresome on the subject of the big two-place aircraft they flew, but probably they had reason to be proud. The F-4 Phantom was easily the greatest fighter plane of the decade, destined to take its place in the Air Force hall of fame alongside such famous craft as the Thunderbolt, the Mustang, and the Sabre. Crammed with sophisticated electronics gear, armed with both missiles and can-non, it could go more than twice as fast as the speed of sound. And thanks to its impressive ordnance-carrying capacity (up to sixteen thousand pounds), the Phantom was as formidable in ground attack as it was in its pure fighter role.

Hambleton watched the monstrous jets howl in at mind-boggling speed, hugging the deck. They put in their ordnance with precise accuracy, clobbering the hill he had pointed out.

Hambleton saw one of the heavy guns, a 100-mm, actually leap into the air. A direct hit—"Banzai!" he muttered. "That'll teach you bastards to shoot down defenseless old navigators!"

"How we all doin' down there?" asked the jets' leader.

"Stand by, Crabtree. Birddog to Bat Twenty-one. How are we doing?"

Hambleton transmitted. "Birddog from Bat. Doin' fine. Make next pass a hundred yards east of the last one."

"Roger, Bat. Nice having the coach right on the field calling the shots."

"That's a matter of opinion"

Hambleton listened as Birddog relayed his message to the jets' leader. They came in again. And again. From his vantage point Hambleton could direct the assault with deadly accuracy. Even six large tanks covered with camouflage netting at the side of the road were quickly reduced to scrap metal.

In pass after pass the Phantoms barreled in over the target with their loads of destruction. Dropping low like great sinister birds of prey, they unleashed their miniature hurricanes of fire and steel, then whined back up into the heavens. When the last of their ordnance had been expended the F-4 leader bade the FAC a cheery good-bye and the whole dark flock thundered off to the nest from which they had come.

It was again comparatively quiet, but through the ringing in his ears Hambleton could hear the crackling of fires and the muted moaning of men. As a participant in the attack, Hambleton's adrenaline had been pumping overtime. He had been calling the shots to Birddog—"Make another pass a hundred yards left of the last one," or "Repeat that last strike on hill thirty-two, but fifty yards more to the right to get that bunker." He had reveled in the joy of the gladiator, meting out punishment to an adversary who had punished him.

But now, in the quiet aftermath of the battle, his glands no longer gearing him for combat, he felt a strange aftershock as he surveyed the carnage before him. The twisted carcasses of metal monsters were stewn along the roads before him as far as he could see. The intersection was a burning, bomb-cratered funeral pyre sending billowing smoke and the acrid smell of cordite into the sky. Bodies were strewn along the roads, strange, unreal marionettes with severed strings.

He shook his head numbly. As a professional military flyer he was no stranger to military operations or the grim ravages of war. But until now his participation—as deadly dangerous as it had been—had always been detached from the grisly reality of close-quarter ground combat. Wrapped in a clean, pristine aluminum envelope, he had done his fighting miles above the scene. It had almost been a computer game—his electronic sophistication matched against that of the enemy in the crisp blue skies of the upper atmosphere.

Down here it was no game. Down here were the guts, gore, and grime of war. Here were the end results of man's inhumanity to man honed to the highest degree of technical expertise. The science of combat had been elevated to the highest art—if art it was to efficiently turn healthy human beings into fertilizer!

Hambleton felt his stomach churning. Maybe he was going to be sick. He turned away and ran a clammy hand across his face.

"Bat Twenty-one from Birddog."

He picked up his radio. "Come in, Birddog. Bat Twenty-one."

"Quite a little show, eh, Bat?"

"Roger. Quite a little show."

"Much action down there?"

"Quiet. Gomers are licking their wounds."

"You're a helluva coach. We just might leave you down there."

"Please, no favors."

"We got a problem."

"Oh? I didn't know we had any problems."

"Gooks bound to know you got a ringside seat observing their activities. They're going to double their efforts to get to you."

"Then I suggest we double our efforts to get me the hell out of here."

"Exactly our plan. Rescue choppers are airborne. Have your flares ready. But don't pop smoke until you hear from Jolly Green. You can monitor them on this frequency."

"*Roger!*" His nausea eclipsed by suddenly soaring spirits. Hambleton dug out his flares. There was an open area not far away in which a chopper could land. When he got the word he would dash out there and ignite his flares.

Hugging the ground, he listened for the familiar clattering sound of helicopter rotors. There would be two coming in—one for rescue, the other a gunship for its protection. And of course there would be his Birddog above the scene to call in the jets or the Sandys to shoot up anything that moved while he sprinted for the pickup point. Hot damn! He would soon be ordering a tall, frosty beer....

In the distance he heard them coming. Hambleton poised, ready to sprint. He had his radio volume turned up so as not to miss any transmissions from the rescue-chopper pilot. Closer and closer the sound came, and then, craning his neck up over the foliage, he could see them. Coming in low and fast. He flexed his leg muscles, ready to go....

Suddenly hades erupted. Antiaircraft opened up in front of

him, 23-mm, 37-mm, and 57-mm automatic guns spraying a wall of iron into the air. Small-arms fire began banging like popcorn.

"What the bloody hell!" Hambleton shouted. He spun around, dazed. Where in God's name had those guns come from? Nothing could have survived the aerial attack just delivered on the intersection. Yet here were guns sending up a curtain of fire he could barely see through....

From the villages to the east! Guns dug in among the villages that had been spared by the fighters to avoid killing civilians; guns heavily entrenched and camouflaged, out of sight of fighters or the FAC.

There was absolutely no way for the choppers to get through the barrier of lead being thrown up. Yet on they came, chuffing toward him! He could see the gray smoke from the machine guns firing in the lead gunship.

Summoned by Birddog, a gaggle of F-4's came wheeling down out of the sun, trying to pinpoint the guns, firing at flashes, frustrated and unable to deliver a full-fledged attack on the off-limits villages.

The choppers were less than a mile away when Hambleton heard a crisp transmission that froze his blood.

"Birddog from Jolly Green. Sorry. Picked up a round in my engine. Aborting."

Despair hung like lead on Birddog's acknowledgment. "Roger, Jolly Green."

Hambleton watched, the emotion draining from him. The choppers banked over sharply and clattered back in the direction from which they had come. The rescue chopper was trailing a wisp of blue smoke. As the Jolly Greens disappeared from view, the F-4's broke off their attack to escort the helicopters back to their base.

Several minutes passed before Birddog broke radio silence. "Bat Twenty-one from Birddog. Sorry as hell, Bat. But we'll get you out. Can you dig in for the night?"

Hambleton tried to muster a cheerfulness that died aborning. "Roger, Birddog."

"Good man. Keep in touch. Birddog out."

Feeling nothing, Hambleton unconsciously stuffed his flares back into his survival vest. He could only return to his hole and dig in. As he prepared to sneak back through the brush, he took one last look at the desolation of the highway intersection.

But it was desolate no longer. Incredibly, the place was teeming with activity. Like a busy anthill that had had its top kicked off, the whole area was swarming with parties of soldiers. To accommodate the incoming traffic from the north, the roads were already being cleared. Burning and bombed-out trucks and weapons carriers were being shoved to the side of the road, the injured and dead thrown into trucks, and a new stream of traffic was threading its way through the wreckage. Troops were everywhere, barking out orders and acknowledgments in shrill Vietnamese.

Hambleton swore. It was going to take some doing to sanitize this area. Like trying to plug up the Mississippi with a cork. If new personnel and equipment were already swarming in after the blistering Armageddon of only a few minutes ago, how in hell would they ever get a Jolly Green in to pick him up?

He dragged himself back through the underbrush to his hole. Numbly he crawled in, unholstered his .38, donned his mosquito netting, and covered himself up. His tongue was dry and his lips were parched. He was incredibly thirsty. It had been over twenty-four hours since he had had anything to drink.

Toward dusk, the ground fog started stealing back in, rolling across the fields and slipping silently among the trees. It found Hambleton's hole and settled gently into it, like some melancholy emblem of his own sinking spirits.

The Third Day

Captain Dennis Clark herded his tall frame through the door of the flight-line maintenance shack, went over to the coffee urn and poured himself a cup of coffee. He took it over to the broken-down sofa that served as the flight-line roost, sat down, and hiked his cowboy boots up on the champagne crate that served as a coffee table. He was bushed.

"Hey, Denny!" Clark looked up to see the short figure of Jake Campbell swinging through the door.

"How they hangin', Jake?"

"Ops said you just landed. Come on."

"Where we going?"

"To the club. Where else?"

"Can't do it, Jake. Going up again. Soon as they refuel my bird."

Campbell checked his watch. "You crazy, man? Hell, it's after midnight. There's a big party going on over at the club. Got a couple girls from the Special Service's troupe corraled in the bar. We're having a farewell party."

"Outstanding. Who's leaving?"

Campbell gave him a slap on the shoulder. "You are, old stud. Your orders came in this afternoon."

Clark put down his cup. "Say again?"

"I repeat. Your orders came in this afternoon."

"Back to the States?"

"Right on. Back to the land of the big BX. You've finished your tour in this garden paradise, old man."

"The hell!"

"As your old roommate and only friend, I've taken the liberty of booking you on a flight leaving for the States tomorrow." He looked at his watch again. "Correction. Make that today. Sorry I couldn't get you on a flight leaving sooner."

"I'll be go to hell."

"Undoubtedly. Now will you come with me? You wouldn't believe the redhead I've got staked out that's panting for your ugly frame."

Clark unzipped a pocket of his flight suit and pulled out a cigarette. "So I've actually completed a tour in this ball-crunchin' madhouse."

"That you have, m'lad. You can kiss your little Birddog good-bye forever. It's back to the land of milk and honey. Where all the women have round eyes and big boobs."

"Where am I going?"

"Nellis. Flying F-one-elevens. How does that grab ya?"

"You're kidding!"

"Sex-mad I am. A kidder I ain't."

Clark smacked his leg with the palm of his hand. "God *damn!*"

"Ain't too shabby."

He pulled out his lighter and lit his cigarette. "F-one-elevens. The switchblade. Must be some mistake. How did the Air Force screw up? That's what I requested."

"And Nellis Air Patch, Nevada. Right in the backyard of Lost Wages. With acres of show girls with legs that go clear up to their assets."

Clark grinned at his roommate and took a deep drag from his cigarette. "But you'll have to cancel my plane reservation, Jake. Can't leave quite yet."

Campbell cocked his head. "Say again your message. You're coming in garbled."

"I appreciate it, Jake. But not just yet. I'm still on a job."

"But your orders—"

"I've got leave coming. I'll take it here until I've finished what I'm doing."

"My God, man, you're exasperating! Just what the hell is so bloody important to keep you in this Black Hole of Calcutta?"

"A gent by the name of Iceal E. Hambleton. Lieutenant Colonel, United States Air Force."

"Hambleton. He's the nav who was shot down?"

"Affirmative."

"You know him?"

"Never met him."

Campbell looked intently into the face of his roommate. "I don't think I understand."

"Nothing to understand. There's a fifty-three-year-old man holed up in the hottest spot in Vietnam. And the old geezer's got lots of guts. As long as he can hang on, I'm hanging in there with him."

"Look, ole buddy. You ain't the only FAC pilot in Vietnam. We got a squadron full of them. Some have been out there keeping an eye on Hambleton whenever you had to come back for a refill."

Clark stopped him with a raised palm. "I know that, Jake. But humility aside, you and I know that I'm the most experienced O-2 throttle jock over here. Plus I know the sector that Hambleton's down in like the back of my hand. What's more, I've worked with about every fighter flight leader over here and know them on a first-name basis. I know what they can do, and they know how I operate. A team effort like this can make a lot of difference in a ticklish rescue operation. Agreed?"

"Agreed. But you got a head full of large agates. If I had a reprieve of sentence from this cruddy war...."

"Tell the gals I'm sorry to miss the party." Clark rose, snuffed out his cigarette, and picked up his clipboard. "The bird should be refueled by now."

Campbell shook his head. "All right, you bullheaded bastard. No use arguing with a fireplug. But I think this screwy war's gotten to you. You need a shrink."

Clark grinned. "No doubt about it."

"I'll see ya later. You don't mind if I go back and continue celebrating your farewell party?"

"Be my guest."

"Too bad you ain't going somewhere."

It was well past midnight. Hambleton was lying in his hole wide awake. He had tried to sleep, but he couldn't help licking his dry lips, and the perspiration salt only made him thirstier. Further, there was a discontented lion growling around in his empty stomach.

But at best, his sleep would have been fitful. With the advent of darkness the night-bombing capability of the bombers and fighters became effective, and from time to time a strike would come in. The whistling shrill of the Phantoms was easy to recognize, but he could only guess at some of the others.

Whenever he heard one of the friendlies thundering in on a strike he automatically braced himself, for he knew he would have to abide the frightening fire of the antiaircraft batteries surrounding him. After each firing he would sit there gritting his teeth, waiting for the pieces of pot metal from the exploding flak to rain down upon him. He had learned to burrow down into his hole leaving only his helmet sticking above the ground, with an alacrity that would send a mole looking to its laurels.

During a night strike the ground fire opened up unmercifully. Guns exploded everywhere, lighting the sky with an orange brilliance that snatched at the darkness. It would appear the Communists were just shooting blind, that whenever they heard the sound of aircraft they rose up and flailed their ammunition in every direction just on the off chance of hitting something. But Hambleton knew better. The Communists did not have to take random potshots, they had sophisticated radar guidance and they knew exactly at what altitude the AF planes were flying. Their Russian equipment was in some cases superior to that of the Americans. It was undoubtedly some new technological achievement that had enabled them to bring their SAMs so far south so quickly, thus destroying his own airplane.

It was this more than anything else that caused Hambleton deep concern for the FAC pilots, one or another of whom had been droning overhead virtually all night. It was as if the North Vietnamese were bent on eliminating the cocky little FACs, the sole link between the downed flyer and the deadly fighter-bombers.

The FAC pilots were something else, Hambleton mused. It was well known that you had to be slightly demented to be one. No sane man would think of spending most of his time over enemy territory, mostly deep behind their lines, in an unarmed, unprotected prop-driven airplane. No way. In pursuit of their duties of calling and marking enemy targets for the Air Force and the Infantry, FACs had to run the risk of being the target for everything from slingshots to SAM missiles. Their only protection was coming in low under the enemy radar and surveillance nets—

often below treetop level—to mark the targets, then to skedaddle like spit on a hot stove. Their stock in trade was a fearless, reckless cunning combined with the element of surprise. Not only were they a foolhardy group of pilots, but at the liar's dice table they were to be avoided at all costs.

Shortly after two A.M. things quieted down. It was almost peaceful. Hambleton was just about to drop off when through the silence loomed a different noise. It was the sound of voices!

He stirred to a sitting position, listening hard. He could faintly hear people talking excitedly. The noise seemed to be coming from the villages, and he took careful note of the lights that pinpointed three hamlets within his range of vision, one to the east, one to the south, and one barely visible in the southwest.

The voices were becoming louder. He crawled out of his hole for a better vantage point. Then he saw them, dimly visible in the glow of flashlights—a group of people fanning out from the villages to congregate at the edge of the rice paddies. He could just make out the uniforms of North Vietnamese regulars interspersed among the villagers. They seemed to be conducting some type of meeting.

As he watched nervously the gathering started spreading out into the paddies. Good God! Were they going to search for him? At this ungodly hour? They came toward him, sweeping away the darkness with swinging beams of their lights. He began to perspire. His palm, holding the butt of his snub-nosed revolver, became slippery. He wiped it off on his flying suit and regripped the .38, ready to shoot.

The searchers continued their exploration for over an hour. They would come up to—but never cross—an invisible line out in the middle of the paddies—his land-mined "Maginot Line." At last they gathered in a large group, talked briefly, then began splitting up and heading back to the villages.

Hambleton mopped the sweat from his face. Obviously they knew roughly where he was holed up. The gravel mining by the Sandys had marked the circular perimeter of the area in which he was hiding. The enemy knew about gravel, and had it spotted now. That had probably been the purpose of this exercise. The soldiers had pressed the villagers into service to help them define the gravel area and make sure it surrounded their prey. But what they intended to do next Hambleton could only guess.

He ducked back into his hole and checked in with the FAC pilot on station. Upon being informed that another rescue attempt would be made at dawn, he signed off. Yet somehow even this news failed to cheer him up. In a somber mood, he curled into a fetal position and tried to go to sleep.

Hambleton slept fitfully for almost an hour. Then again he was awakened by the grumble of heavy machinery. He sat for a moment listening and mustering his senses. A strange light seemed to be flickering in the distance, to the north, toward the intersection. He wiped the sleep from his eyes, then crawled out of his hole to investigate.

Peering from his observation knoll, he was surprised to see that burning flares were responsible for the light—small flares, little larger than the fireball of a Roman candle, firing one at a time and at irregular intervals. His hand went instinctively to his .38. Were they searching for him again?

No. No one was heading his way. There were soldiers, but they were concerned only with the busy highway. They were moving equipment and supplies along the main arterial, taking advantage of the darkness. He blinked, accustoming his eyes to the faint light, and then slowly, he began to understand what was going on. It was a long convoy of trucks bumper to bumper, their headlights off, groping through the dark. The small flares were being lighted by men in the lead vehicle. Each flare would burn for several minutes while the convoy moved, then the men in the front truck would light another and repeat the process. It was a good plan. Any pilot looking for this truck convoy would never find it. If the truck drivers heard a plane coming, they simply would not light the next flare. As simple as that. They were in business.

He studied the operation until he was sure of the *modus operandi,* then he called the FAC. Within minutes came the ominous thunder of approaching Phantoms.

Hambleton hightailed it back to his hole, not wanting to be any closer to the target area than necessary. The fighters' night-bombing capability was pretty accurate, but this was no time to take chances. He burrowed down into his lair, put on his helmet, and steeled himself for the fallout from exploding ack-ack overhead.

Down roared the Phantoms, making several passes, triggering

the god-awful firing of the big guns nearby. It all combined to make a heaving, rocking, crashing inferno that lit up the sky like a million star shells.

Abruptly the attack ceased. When Hambleton's ears quit ringing he could tell the throaty growl of slow-moving trucks had been silenced. He shook the debris from his helmet and once again lay back.

Goddamn, wars were noisy.

Again Hambleton awoke from his catnap with a start.

It was still dark. He checked the radium dial of his watch. Four-twenty. God, how time flew when you were having a ball! He sat up, working his jaws, trying to bring saliva to his dry mouth.

He had been dreaming of a chocolate milkshake. Not that he was all that crazy about chocolate milkshakes, but the cold, creamy liquid gliding down his parched throat had been pure ambrosia. Now he was awake with cracked lips and a tongue furred like an old army blanket.

His stomach let out a plaintive rumble. He had to do something. Even if it was wrong, he had to find something to eat. He had to get nourishment into his body, or when the chopper came in he wouldn't have the strength to run for it.

He made a decision.

During the day he had memorized the surrounding landscape. To the west of his wooded area the land stretched out, looking not unlike the plowed fields of Illinois or Indiana. Instead of cornfields there were rice paddies with ditches around them. Raised paths maybe a foot and a half wide separated the ditches and paddies. Beyond was a good-sized village. Beyond the village were more rice paddies, probably extending as far as the Song Mien Giang River.

In a rice paddy just a short distance from his location, very near the inside perimeter of the gravel, he had spotted a little garden. He had been told in survival training that the Vietnamese families often planted a garden in one corner of their rice paddies. Not large, but big enough to provide for the family table between harvests. The one nearby had a corn patch, and he thought he had recognized other native plants—taro, watermelon, pineapple, and red pepper.

Taro, the starchy, tuberous root which was a main staple of the Vietnamese diet, didn't really turn him on. He had tasted poi at a Hawaiian luau, and had swiftly categorized it as having the same tantalizing flavor as denture cement. But now, in his condition, even the thought of poi set his gastric juices flowing.

Lying there, scrutinizing the little plot, he lamented the season. It was not the best time of year to go groveling around in a garden. The corn silks had looked slightly tan and the corn appeared to be the only thing that was anywhere near mature. But ripe or not, it did look appetizing.

But he had made the decision; he would go foraging. He knew how. He had done it in his childhood days in Illinois when he and his buddies had gone watermelon stealing in the same kind of feeble moonlight. Only one difference. Instead of a farmer with a pepper-loaded shotgun, there was antiaircraft fire coming out of the center of the nearby village. That battery had been largely responsible for the choppers turning back. And those guns weren't loaded with pepper.

He called the FAC. The pilot responded immediately. "Come in, Bat Twenty-one."

"Don't you ever sleep?"

"Sleep is bad for my insomnia. What can I do for you?"

"Hungry. Little garden nearby. Going shopping."

There was a pause as this information was considered. When he came back there was a note of concern in his voice. "Roger, Bat. I'll alert the Sandys. We'll fly top cap. Any trouble, click your transmitter at three-second intervals."

"Wilco."

"And Bat, be careful. Make like Tiny Tim. Check in when you return."

"Wilco. Bat Twenty-one out." Hambleton thought for a moment. Make like Tiny Tim? And then he understood. Have to tiptoe through the tulips. The mine field.

He could feel his heart hammering as he crawled out of his hole. He was willing to leave his sanctuary, his safe haven. Still, although it was a dark night, with scudding clouds that mostly blocked out the wisp of a moon, he would be exposed. He began to have second thoughts. And then another low growl from his midriff confirmed his decision.

He removed his heavy survival vest. He shouldn't need it and it would only weigh him down. He took his knife and his radio, placed his other belongings in his hole, and carefully covered them with branches.

Compass in hand, he crawled to the edge of his cover. Then, crouching low, he started stalking his objective. Since he not only had to reach the garden but find the hole upon his return, he started counting his steps. One...two...three...Compass heading exactly one hundred and fifty-eight degrees.

Nervous sweat plastered his flying suit to his skin. The garden plot should be just inside the land-mined strip, but it was marginal at best, and there was no telling where some of the mines had rolled to upon impact. His eyes stinging with perspiration, he stared intently at the dark ground before each footfall...checking his compass...counting his steps. He pulled up short, spotting what might be a land mine—couldn't really tell in the dark—but giving it a wide berth.

He paused from time to time, listening, reconnoitering the area. To the southwest, over a little rise, was another small village. Straight west beyond the rice paddies was a group of three or four gray buildings he had not seen before. There was a large stone gate entry to the area, probably a place of worship. From the rise he could get a different view of the main arterial road. He could distinguish the outlines of several camouflaged tanks parked under a tree, and he made a mental note of their position. Birddog would be interested.

Skirting along the ditch he came across a berry patch. Quickly he frisked one of the larger bushes, and his hands yielded several red berries. Remembering the rule of survival school, he squeezed the juice in the palm of his hand and touched it with his tongue. He didn't recognize the taste, but it was sweet, meaning it should be edible. Delighted, he stripped the nearest bushes, gathering several handfuls of the fruit, which he stuffed into his pockets.

After another thirty yards he found himself at the edge of the garden and made a dash for the spindly cornfield at its far corner. Ducking into the protection of the stalks he squatted, caught his breath, and listened. No gooks! No mines! So far so good. Only the comforting drone of the aircraft overhead permeated the predawn stillness.

Quietly he moved from one stalk to another, snapping the largest ear from each stalk. Three ears, he told himself. That's all. From different stalks so as not to indicate he'd been there. With his limit stuffed into the pockets of his flight suit, he started creeping back toward the corner of the garden, the point of his directional bearing.

As he did so, he tripped over a little mound. Cursing silently, he picked himself up, discovering in the process a small row of pineapples. Reaching down he plucked one, about the size of a hand grenade, and stuffed in into his pocket. Then, compass in hand, he prepared to retrace his steps. Let's see—the reciprocal of the heading that had brought him to the corner of the garden would be three three-eight degrees. He sighted this heading, then started off, counting his steps.

Stealthily, crouched almost doubled over, squatting occasionally to listen, he made his way back to the wooded area. Now, if he had stayed precisely on his compass course, had properly counted his steps, his hole should be about...here. He poked around with his hands in the dark.

No hole.

My God! If he couldn't find his hole he was in deep trouble. All his materials of survival—flares, gun, and everything—were in that hole. He felt the hairs on his neck rise. Stop it! He mustn't panic.

He forced himself to relax until his panting stopped. Then he marked his spot and started walking around it in ever-increasing circles.

Three minutes later he stepped into his hole.

He stripped away the brush cover, saw with relief that his belongings were just as he had left them, then crawled back into his haven. Even his caterpillar was safe. He gave a moment of thanks. He had successfully debarked from his sanctuary, and by virtue of cunning and his navigational skills he had returned safe and sound. He grinned to himself as he recalled the old saw fliers used on returning from a mission: "Once again science and skill have triumphed over ignorance and superstition." No one ever mentioned luck.

He checked in on the radio. There was obvious relief in the voice of the pilot as he acknowledged. "Good show, Bat Twenty-one. We were worried."

"No sweat. Now if you'll excuse me, dinner's waiting."

"Bon appétit, Bat. Listening, out."

Gently Hambleton removed the berries from the pockets of his flying suit and placed them in his helmet. Then he took one ear of corn and put the other two in a pocket of his survival vest for safekeeping. With the care of a man restoring an old painting, he delicately peeled the husks off the ear of corn, and picked off each silk. Then, after carefully burying the leavings, he settled back in his hole, picked up the ear of corn in his grimy hands, and began nibbling down the rows, a kernel at a time, reveling in the pleasant taste of the sweet milk. When he had finished with the corn, he solemnly proceeded to eat the cob, grinding it down to a pulp fine enough to swallow.

Then came the fruit. One by one he consumed the berries, first savoring them in his mouth, then crushing them with his tongue, delighting in the squirting juice that bathed his mouth and provided much-needed liquid to his body.

But the pineapple was something else. It was as green and hard as the hand grenade it resembled. It defied all of his efforts to cut it with the knife, so it went into the hole along with the corn husks and silk.

He lay back and patted his stomach. He longed for a cigarette to top off his repast. God, would a Marlboro taste good. But he had to knock it off. He didn't need a cigarette. He had food in his stomach. Look at the bright side! Count his blessings! Relax! Perhaps a little after-dinner nap would put everything back into proper perspective.

He shut his eyes and starting composing a military letter to the Surgeon General about cigarettes.

But sleep still would not come. The sullen booming of far-off guns was scarcely a lullaby, and the introduction of food to his shrunken stomach had given him an unpleasant cramp.

This damned war! He wished he could pull the switch. No man had any business being in this ridiculous position, least of all a guy who was on the threshold of his golden years. It wasn't fair.

He tried to switch mental channels. Here he was, a fifty-three–year–old poop, homesick and feeling sorry for himself like some kid. Idiotic…But why not? Stuck in this dark, grubby, hole. He hadn't shaved for three days and his beard itched. His flying suit was so filthy he could have planted rice in it. He smelled like a goat and his teeth felt furry. Above all, he was weak, hungry and genuinely frightened.

Why had he been singled out to be put through this terrifying, nerve-jangling, miserable wringer? There was nothing he had done to God, or anyone else, that merited this kind of punishment. Oh sure, he could have gone to church more. But he wasn't an atheist. Or even an agnostic. He did believe in God. And he subscribed to the Ten Commandments. And the Golden Rule.

Foolishly, he began to enumerate his sins and the shortcomings of his character. He rehearsed adolescent escapades and the pecadillos of young manhood, assuring himself at each step along the way that he had never done anything to deserve this kind of retribution.

Even as a husband he hadn't strayed too far. His fondness for gambling seldom exceeded quarter-limit poker, his craving for Manhattans seldom got him into trouble, he paid bills on time and he worked hard at his job. He liked the military life—especially the flying. When he had graduated as a smart-assed second lieutenant in the Army Air Corps in 1945, he had boasted that he would stay in for five years or five stars, whichever came first. He had later lowered his sights to staying in and merely becoming the best goddamn navigator in the Air Force. He may not have become the best, but he felt he was right up among them. And evidently the Air Force felt the same way, for his hard work and sense of professionalism had merited him not only a regular commission, but commendable progression through the ranks.

It certainly wasn't a question of other women. Unlike some of the younger officers, he just didn't see any sense in going out for a hot dog when he had filet mignon waiting for him at home. He had tried to be a good husband over the years, and it hadn't been difficult. Gwen had more than done her share to make the marriage work. He still found her as charming and desirable as she had been when they were first married. There had been no children, but that apart, theirs had been a near-perfect marriage.

Gwen. God, how he missed her! How he would love to...

Hambleton! You bloody, weeping bastard! Get hold of yourself!

With an effort he pulled himself upright. He would do something constructive. He sat on the edge of his hole and stretched his muscles. Then he dug out his first-aid kit, opened it, and stripped the mosquito netting gauntlet from his left hand. He took off the old bandage and inspected the wound. It was a nasty gash that should have had stitches, but at least it wasn't infected. He put on a fresh bandage and taped it up.

He replaced the contents of the first-aid kit and tucked it away in its niche in his hole. In the faintly gathering light he could see the early-morning fog rolling across the paddies toward him. It was going to be damp. Probably damp enough to deposit some dew on the leaves. Maybe even a few raindrops. He rummaged in his hole and produced the rubber map. After spreading it out on the leaves of a nearby bush, he got his empty plastic water container and put it where it would be handy. Then he crawled back into his hole, covered himself up, shut his eyes, and murmured a short prayer.

Colonel John Walker was heavyset, brusque, efficient, and the Commander of the 355th TAC Fighter Wing—Hambleton's outfit. At the moment he was with several of his staff officers who were in the wing briefing room at the Korat Royal Thai Air Force Base. The men were gathered around a wall-sized terrain map of the area in which Hambleton had been shot down.

As the officers talked, Major Sam Piccard, the wing intelligence officer, walked into the briefing room. Carrying a classified intelligence folder, he approached Walker. "May I have a moment, Colonel?" he asked, removing the stem of an old, stained meerschaum from his mouth.

Walker nodded, and separated from the group with Piccard. "What is it, Sam?"

"We've just received some bad news, about Hambleton, Colonel."

Walker grunted. "Let's have it."

"An intelligence report just came in. Apache Control monitored a North Vietnamese radio broadcast. The Communists know who Hambleton is."

"Oh, Christ!"

"They found the wreckage of the plane."

"I know." Walker exhaled loudly. "So now they know our downed flyer's name and rank. And the fact that he punched out of an EB-sixty-six. Which would naturally make him an electronic counter-measure expert. That's bad enough. Do they know the rest?"

"That he was in the Strategic Air Command?"

"That he was assistant DCO of a SAC Missile Wing before he went back to the cockpit."

"That's hard to say, sir. North Vietnamese intelligence is spotty, but as you know, they come up with some surprises."

"Being a missile man, the Russians will probably have a dossier on him an inch thick." Walker mulled it over. "So this opens up a whole new keg of worms. We've not only got a downed flyer in the enemy camp, which is bad enough, but a man walking around with a head full of top-secret war plans."

"If they find out they'll damn near stop the war to get him."

"You better believe it." Deep in thought, Walker moved across the room to join his staff gathered around the map. "Gentlemen," he said flatly, "we've got to get Hambleton the hell out of there. The fit has just hit the shan."

The Fourth Day

Hambleton was awakened by a languid sun poking its way through the veil of fog. He looked around, rubbing burning eyes, and swore. Damn weather! Was it going to be a repetition of yesterday, when the visibility was restricted to less than a quarter of a mile?

He smacked his lips, trying to get saliva pumping into his dry mouth, then reached out and checked the rubber map spread out on the bush. It was beaded with the morning's dew, as were the leaves on the bush. He mopped the moisture up with his handkerchief, sucked out as much as he could, then rubbed the damp cloth over his face and the back of his neck. Finally, he ran his finger in a circular motion over his teeth. His toilet complete, he was ready for the new day.

He hoped it would be a lot better than yesterday. During the daylight hours he had done little but monitor the hourly reports from Birddog, receiving the latest weather sequences. All day the ceiling had remained lower than a midget's ass. The Jolly Greens didn't even get airborne, let alone attempt a rescue. But according to the weather prophets, today was supposed to be better. The front was supposed to move out.

At least he had accomplished something. He hadn't just sat on his hands all day and soured himself with more self-pity. In the best traditions of survival he had busied himself with an objective. Maybe his project would not seem much of an accomplishment to a lot of people, but again, not many people had spent three days sitting in a hole, deep in enemy territory.

He reached out for his project and picked it up. He removed the little thatched roof and checked on Chester. The caterpillar seemed to be enjoying the little house Hambleton had patiently woven for him from strips of corn husks. About the size of a strawberry box, it had turned out quite well. At least its occupant seemed to be thriving, not only protected from the elements, but also from the gimlet-eyed birds.

Hambleton put in several fresh leaves and replaced the roof. Yes, both he and Chester were going to survive. Make the best of an unfortunate situation.

In the distance he heard again the clank-clank of heavy tanks. It was going to be another busy day at the office. He emerged from his hole and groped his way through the undergrowth to his vantage point on the little knoll that overlooked the intersection. The ground fog was thinning fast; being dissipated by the morning sun. Hot damn! Maybe today would be rescue day.

Lying on his belly, he watched the tanks—T-54 heavies and PT-76 amphibious lights—coming down from the DMZ in a long line. On reaching the intersection the monsters separated, some going east, others west. He crawled back to his hole to notify Birddog.

In a low voice he relayed the information to the FAC. Then in a matter of minutes the F-4's came howling in overhead. Very businesslike, he crossed his arms and waited for the surrounding antiaircraft batteries to open up on the attacking jets. Now, almost without thinking, he put on his helmet before the shrapnel from the exploding AA shells rained down around him.

After the fighter attack had silenced the grumble of the tanks, he again whispered to Birddog: "There ought to be an easier way to make a living."

"What's the matter, Bat? Getting tired of being the number-one duck in our shooting gallery?"

"Some of the fun has gone out of it."

"Why didn't you say so? We'll yank you out of there."

"Wonderful idea."

"Get out your flares. The Jolly Greens are coming. But first duck your head. We're gonna play you a little tune."

"Roger." Hambleton knew what was coming. They were going to bring in all the air power they could muster to neutralize the area before the choppers came in. He dug into his hole as far as he could and pulled Chester in after him.

Down they thundered. For fifteen minutes the air around him

sounded like the climax of the *1812 Overture* gone amok. Birddog was the conductor, leading the overture of death from the podium of his tiny 0-2. Hambleton shut his eyes, clenched his jaws, and placed his hands over his ears. But the thundering, earth-shaking symphony of bombardment came in loud and clear. The whining F-105's were the wind instruments, the C-130 gunships the snare drums, the hurtling F-4's climaxing the overture with the cymbal crash of their cluster bombs.

For a quarter of an hour that seemed like an eternity Hambleton rolled with the shock waves, jumped with the concussions, and spat dirt. Then it ended as quickly as it had begun.

He shook the dust out of his hair, wiped the grit from his eyes, and blinked. He was still in one piece. He looked around him. All he could see was the dust and smoke of the aftermath. He waited for things to settle and his ears to quit buzzing, then he checked in with the orbiting FAC pilot.

"You play quite a tune, Birddog."

"It grows on you. You're gonna have to pull in your welcome mat for a bit, Bat. Complications. Will get back to you within the hour."

Frowning, Hambleton clicked an acknowledgment. Complications? He hadn't liked the worried tone of Birddog's usually upbeat voice. What the hell could be the complication? He rose up and looked around him. There were several crackling fires but nothing seemed to be moving. Nothing. As far as the eye could see. Even the villages were quiescent.

He looked up and scanned the sky. The ground fog had completely burned off and there were only a few puffy altocumulus off to the east. Weather was perfect. If ever the Jolly Greens could come in, this was the time. What was the holdup? Knowing the blood-and-guts courage of the SAR rescue teams, it had to be something serious. The guns dug into the villages? Even most of these had been pinpointed and neutralized by the fighters. The weather was CAVU and the opposition was hanging on the ropes. What were the complications?

Damn, what he wouldn't give for a cigarette!

In the briefing room of the Korat Command Post several wing staff officers were gathered around a table on which were spread a series of aerial reconnaissance photos. Colonel Walker looked up as Captain Dennis Clark walked in, wearing a flying suit wet with perspiration.

"How's it going, Clark?"

"Hot, sir," said Clark.

"It's been one of those days. How was Hambleton when you left him?"

"Confused and dejected."

Walker looked grim. "Hell of a note! We might have yanked him out of there by this time if it hadn't happened. Does he know about the OV-10 FAC that was shot down near his area?"

"No."

"Try to explain to him why the Jolly Greens didn't go in to get him after the bombardment. If he knows they were on another rescue mission, he'll understand."

"Wilco, sir. What's the latest?"

"We're still putting the pieces together. Looks like the pilot went down with his plane. But the observer seems to have gotten out okay. At least we got the area around him sanitized. How did it look out there?"

Clark moved to the terrain map on the briefing room wall. He pointed to a spot about four miles east of Hambleton's position. "He's down in some trees right about here. The SAR Sandys and our jets really clobbered the area around him, but it's still too hot to get the Jolly Greens in. They tried three times."

Walker studied the area. "Christ, we can sure pick some great spots to auger in! Smack in the middle of a battleground. Is the area as hot as Hambleton's?"

"No. The observer is more isolated. Not as close to a major arterial intersection as Colonel Hambleton is."

Walker shook his head. "This is going to take some strategy. Now we've got *two* men down in the hottest spots of the war. The staff is working on several ideas now. How about giving them your latest eyewitness intelligence."

"Yes, sir."

"Oh, Clark. One more thing. I just learned that your orders came through. Assigning you back to the States."

"Yes, sir."

"Then why aren't you on your way out of here?"

"Got a few odds and ends to clear up first, Colonel. Then I'll start."

"Oh? I didn't know we were now running the Air Force at the convenience of captains."

"No, sir. I've cleared it with my squadron CO. I'm on leave."

Walker looked quizzically at the tall pilot. "Did I understand you correctly? You're taking leave—*here?*"

"Yes, sir. Until, as I say, I get a few odds and ends cleared up. Besides, I'm crazy about the mess hall."

Walker grunted. "I knew FAC pilots were all a little shell-shocked. But you're ready for the rubber room."

"So my roommate keeps informing me."

"Going to F-one-elevens is a pretty choice assignment. They won't keep it open for you if you don't make your reporting date."

"I realize that."

"OK. You can stay on the mission. But," he looked narrowly at Clark, "I want you to get your crew rest. According to the Ops reports you've almost been flying around the clock."

"Not quite, sir. Been getting my beauty rest. Catnaps while they refuel my plane, some here, some there."

"You heard me. I said *crew rest.* You've got to stay sharp. Some isn't enough. A lot of those fog banks are stuffed with large mountains. And I don't want another downed pilot to worry about."

"Yes, sir." Clark excused himself and went over to the staff officers huddled around the reconnaissance photos.

Major Sam Piccard looked up and squinted through the smoke of his meerschaum. "Hi, Denny. Understand you've had a busy day. How goes it on the front lines?"

"Things could be better."

"They sure could. Did I ever tell you what Mussolini said about war?"

"No, Sam, but I have a feeling you're going to."

Piccard tamped his pipe. "War alone brings up to its highest tension all human energy and puts the stamp of nobility upon the peoples who have the courage to face it."

"That's beautiful."

"How does it feel to be noble and courageous?"

"No wonder they shot Mussolini."

Piccard grinned. "You have a point."

"Before I give you my intelligence report, answer me a question."

"Shoot."

"About that downed FAC observer. Who is he? Has he been positively identified?"

"He has. A lieutenant. Name of Clark. You don't have any relatives flying over here?"

"None that I know of."

"You'd be in good company if your were related to this one. His first name's Mark."

"Not Mark Clark? The son of—"

"That's right."

Hambleton was lying on his stomach on his observation knoll making mental notes of the enemy's troop movements on the highway when he heard the buzzing of the FAC plane overhead. He snapped on his radio.

In terse, guarded language the pilot informed him of the reason for the aborted rescue attempt. If not cheered, Hambleton was at least relieved. It was one thing to think his rescuers had abandoned him. It was another to learn that they had been given an alternate, priority mission in an attempt to aid a downed fellow airman.

"Hang in, Bat," said Birddog. "We're lining up our ducks at the head shed. A plan is being worked out. Weather's supposed to hold good. It won't be long now."

"Roger, Birddog. And thanks." Feeling much better, Hambleton clicked off his radio. Best he return to his hole and condense his enemy-movement report to transmit to Birddog. He rolled over on his back to tuck his radio into the front pocket of his flying suit. Then, the sun feeling warm on his face, he relaxed for a moment in preparation for his journey back to the hole.

Suddenly he froze. What in hell was that? Cautiously he turned his head in the direction of the noise.

His blood turned to ice.

Standing not fifteen feet away was a little Vietnamese boy!

Hambleton blinked in shock. The kid looked about ten years of age, dirty, gaunt, shabbily dressed—his eyes the size of sake cups.

Jesus Christ! Where did that kid come from? What the hell should he do? Make a break and run like hell? No. Not in bright daylight. The smart thing to do was just lie there and play dead. He shut his eyes and tried to look like a convincing corpse.

The boy must have detected some motion in the underbrush and come over to investigate. But how did he get through the mine field? Just luck, making like Tiny Tim? Or because God rides in the hip pockets of children?

Hambleton cracked his lids. God, the kid wasn't alone! A large black dog was bounding around near him. Now he not only had a kid watching him, but also a dog that was going to start barking and bring every gomer in Vietnam.

Sighting Hambleton, the dog stopped short. His tail came almost to a point, stiff as a poker. He sniffed the wind, then looked curiously up at his master. Talking low to the dog, the boy approached, stepping softly through the brush.

Hambleton did his best to simulate rigor mortis. He tried to ignore an insect crossing his cheek, praying that not a muscle would twitch. He knew he had to play dead damn well, or soon he might be.

Then the two were upon him. The lad, carrying a stick, gingerly poked Hambleton's chest. The dog started sniffing at his heels, slowly working up his body. Hambleton watched the boy through slitted lids. He did not dare breathe as the lad reached for the zipper of his pocket that contained his radio.

His radio!

Dear God, he couldn't part with that! Not his lifeline to the FAC pilot and survival. If the boy started to take it, what should he do? Attack the kid? Throttle him? Impossible. Take him hostage? Also impossible. He had enough trouble trying to take care of himself. Then, what?

Sniffing Hambleton's head, the dog suddenly started to growl. A low, ominous rale issued from his throat, and he bared his fangs inches above Hambleton's face. Hambleton felt a splatter of drool drop on his cheek. Sweet Jesus! Was he about to be attacked?

The boy muttered a low Vietnamese command to the mongrel. Reproached, the dog pulled back, but his fangs did not retract. Had the beast detected life in the corpse and was warning his master? Or was the canine just hankering for fresh meat? Whatever it was, the dog's actions had caused the boy to pull back his hand. Then, strangely, the boy straightened up and turned around, issuing orders to the dog. Reluctantly, mongrel heeded master, and the two started off at a lively clip to disappear in the tall brush.

Hambleton lay still, immobile, waiting for the tremors of shock to subside. What had all that been about? Had the kid sensed he was alive? Would he report him? Send the soldiers looking for him? Or would the boy—no stranger to dead bodies in the war zone—merely pass him off as an uninteresting incident? After three days in a stinking flying suit he probably smelled like a corpse.

Or there was a remote possibility that the lad might be from a friendly village that might even bring help?

He dismissed that idea. The victorious tide of battle was heading south. Even friendly villages were occupied by enemy troops. He had seen them. If the kid reported him to *anyone*, his fat was in the fire. Christ on a crutch!

Finally he mustered the strength to rise on his elbows. It might prove helpful if he could see which way the kid had gone. He craned his neck, peering over the underbrush until he could see the nearest village.

The boy and the dog were heading across the rice paddies toward the village. As he approached the inside perimeter of the Maginot Line, the boy stopped. He picked up a stick and hurled it as far as he could across the mined strip toward the village. The dog took out after the stick, with the kid following precisely in his path a safe distance behind. *The kid was using his dog to blaze a trail through the mine field!*

Hambleton shook his head, unbelieving. For a moment a touch of sadness leavened his fear. What the hell was this crazy war doing? Everything in Vietnam seemed to be expendable. Everything and everybody. Including a kid's dog. Had terror and the need to survive undone every virtue—pity, decency, loyalty, love?

His musings were interrupted by the actions of the lad and the dog who had by then miraculously negotiated the mined area. They were heading directly for the nearest hooch at the edge of the village. Hambleton's heart sank. He watched the child run up to a woman hanging clothes in the yard and start chattering a mile a minute. Hambleton could make out much gesticulating, which finally culminated in a hand pointing in his direction. Terminating the conversation, the boy and the woman hurried into the hooch.

His skin crawled. What the hell should he do? Should he make a break for it and run toward his hole, risking exposure, or...

His worst fears were confirmed. Several Vietnamese soldiers

bearing rifles came boiling out of the hooch, led by the boy. The dog accompanied them, barking up a storm. They ran in Hambleton's direction, pulling up just short of the mined area. Hambleton could hear the shrill, excited voices of the soldiers as the lad pointed at the exact spot where he was hiding.

He broke out into a cold sweat. He had to make a break for it. Get back to his hole where he could cover himself up. Get his gun. Could he do it without being seen? They would be watching for any movement, knowing exactly where he was hiding. He *had* to pull himself together and get the hell out of there!

But his limbs would not obey his commands. He could only stoop there, transfixed, watching as the soldiers sent the boy and the dog back to the hooch and then started picking their way through the mine field.

Closer...closer the soldiers came. Thank God the kid hadn't shown them the dog trick. It was obvious they didn't know how the kid had made it through the mine field. They were not relishing their duty. Studying the ground beneath them before each footfall ...treading softly, gingerly...stopping, pausing before each step. In spite of his fear, Hambleton felt a touch of admiration for those poor ground-pounders. God Almighty, they must want him bad to try and negotiate that mine field.

He wiped away sweat puddling on his forehead and dripping down his face. He *had* to do something. The first of the three soldiers seemed to be part way through the mine field. One or all of them could get lucky and make it. His hands shaking, he fumbled with his pocket zipper and pulled out his radio. He clicked it on.

"Birddog! Birddog!" He kept his voice low, fighting to keep it from trembling. "This is Bat Twenty-one. *Come in!*"

"Roger, Bat. Birddog here."

"Gomers. Playing Tiny Tim. Coming this way. A quarter click east of my position."

"Roger, Bat. Understand. Birddog out."

Thank God! Help would soon be on the way. But if they didn't make it in time, he'd better be prepared. He got into a crouching position and unsheathed his knife.

The first of the three soldiers was now reaching the inner boundary of the mine field. Hambleton searched the sky. Where in hell were his defenders? Where were the Sandys and the Phantoms and the F-105's? Another ten yards and the nearest soldier might be clear of the mine field heading his way.

Come on, you mothers!

Finally he heard it. The noise of an inbound plane. It wasn't loud, but was coming fast. Hot damn! Now all hell would break loose. The fighters would roar in spewing their lethal bombardment....

And then he spotted the incoming plane. His jaw flopped open. It was no flight of Phantoms. No gaggle of F-105's. Not even Sandys. It was a lone plane. *It was Birddog!*

The little unarmed mosquito had exploded up behind a hill, the sun glinting off its camouflage paint, its props whining like a harpy's cry.

Hambleton stared in open-mouthed amazement at the little O-2 buzzing in at full throttle. What the hell good was that little FAC plane going to be at a time like this? He glanced down at the soldiers. They had heard it too and had stopped in their tracks, turning to look up. Sweeping in at treetop level, the O-2 came boring on like a hopped-up wasp. There was a flash and then a wisp of smoke from under the wing. As the pilot pulled up a few scant feet above the ground, two white phosphorous marking rockets exploded near the advancing soldiers. The Vietnamese barely had time to squeeze off a round at the attacking plane before they were enveloped in the choking white smoke.

The soldiers panicked. Completely forgetting the mines, they raced back toward the village. It was a mistake. One somehow got back out of the mine field unscathed. A second one almost made it, but he tripped near the outside edge of the mined perimeter. There was a muffled *whomp* beneath his sprawled body. He did not get up. Then the leader ran afoul of one of the hideous instruments. There was a loud percussion and he flopped to the ground screaming.

Hambleton's limbs came to life. Taking advantage of the diversion, he crouched low and sprinted through the underbrush. Minutes later he was back in his hole, frantically covering himself with brush. Hidden, he lay there, panting from the terror and the exertion.

Son of a bitch! As he waited for his pulse to stop pounding, he thought of that wild man upstairs who had pressed an attack armed only with target-marking rockets. Right out of *Dawn Patrol*. Hambleton had never seen anything like it.

It was ten minutes before he had regained enough control to call Birddog. Then he checked in.

"Sorry about the grandstand play there, Bat," said the Birddog pilot. "Saw you had a problem. Wasn't time to round up the zoomies, so I came in myself."

"You're crazy, Birddog."

"In this war it's an asset."

"I owe you."

"I'll collect. Meantime, good news. Back at the ranch the planners got their priorities lined up. Jolly Greens coming in mañana. God willin' and the creek don't rise. Weather guessers predict good weather. Can you hang in one more night?"

"I'll hang in."

"Outstanding. Few minutes the Sandys will be coming in with another load of gravel. Gonna fertilize your tulip field."

"I'm beholden."

"One more thing to brighten your day. Chances are the gooks won't try shelling your position. They want you alive."

"That's comforting. Makes two of us."

"Keep in touch. Birddog listening out."

Hambleton clicked off his radio, lay back in his hole, and closed his eyes as a wave of utter fatigue washed over him.

The doorbell rang. Gwen Hambleton clicked off the television set in the family room and went to the door. It was her closest friend, Marge Wilson.

"Happened to be in the neighborhood, Gwen," lied Marge. "Thought I'd pop by for just a minute. See if you need anything."

"Thanks, Marge. Come in for a cup of coffee."

Marge planted herself on a stool at the kitchen counter while Gwen busied herself with the coffeepot. "Anything new?"

Gwen motioned to a telegram lying on the bar. "That just came. Read it."

Marge removed the telegram from its envelope and read:

MRS. GWENDOLYN HAMBLETON DELIVER DO NOT PHONE
REPORT DELIVERY
REFERENCE MY PREVIOUS COMMUNICATION CONCERNING
THE MISSING STATUS OF YOUR HUSBAND, LT COLONEL ICEAL
E. HAMBLETON.
I REGRET TO INFORM YOU THAT ALL SEARCH AND RESCUE
EFFORTS THUS FAR HAVE BEEN FRUITLESS. VOICE CONTACT
IS BEING MAINTAINED, HOWEVER EFFORTS TO RESCUE HIM
HAVE BEEN NEGATIVE. THE SEARCH HAS BEEN HAMPERED
BY POOR WEATHER AND HEAVY HOSTILE ACTIVITY IN THE
SEARCH AREA. EXTENSIVE SEARCH OPERATIONS ARE BEING
CONTINUED AND WHEN ANY INFORMATION IS RECEIVED
YOU WILL BE NOTIFIED IMMEDIATELY. MAY I AGAIN EX-
TEND MY SINCERE SYMPATHY DURING THIS PERIOD OF
ANXIETY.
BRIG GENERAL K.L. TALLMAN COMMANDER AIR FORCE MIL-
ITARY PERSONNEL CENTER

She replaced the telegram in its envelope. "I'll say this," she
said softly, "the Air Force certainly does its best to keep you
informed."

Gwen nodded. "The casualty officer at Davis-Monthan even
brought me the telephone number of the casualty branch at San
Antonio with instructions to call it any time I want. And the phone
rings constantly. Air Force friends have called from all over the
country. Don Buchholz called this evening from the Pentagon."

"Yes. Ham had a lot of friends."

"*Has* a lot of friends."

Marge groaned inwardly. "Of course. *Has* a lot of friends. And
he'll be seeing them soon."

"Yes. Soon."

As Gwen placed a coffee cup in front of her guest, Marge took
her hand. "Would you like me to stay with you again tonight?"

"No thanks. Not tonight, Marge. I just kind of want to be
alone."

"Are you sure?"

"Yes. You're my dearest friend, Marge, you know that. But
tonight I really would prefer it."

"OK. But call me if you need anything? You know you're
taking this thing like a real trooper, Gwen. Ham will be proud."

"Got to. I'm an Air Force wife. You know the procedure."

"Yes, I know it." Marge was doing her best not to let on to Gwen that she'd noticed how much the hands holding the coffeepot were shaking.

It was dusk, and Hambleton could faintly hear the people in the villages going about their evening chores. Painfully, he crawled out of his hole and peered through the bushes. Funny. Almost like an evening at home in Tucson. People coming home from work. He and Gwen would be having a Manhattan about this time, unwinding, maybe starting the coals for an outdoor barbecue. But then the odor of Vietnamese cooking wafted toward him and his nose wrinkled. He was a long way from Tucson.

Interesting how the villagers could go about their business smack in the middle of a war. They all looked so peaceful. Last week, before they had been engulfed by the North Vietnamese offensive, he would have been able to walk through that village completely unmolested. He would have been approached by the kids, smiled at by the women, bowed to by the old men. But not now. Now they were engulfed by the other side, and their reorientation had already begun.

The poor damned Vietnamese. Like children—curious, friendly, vulnerable. Few of the villagers had much will to fight. Simple survival was their ideology, their honor, and their politics. The political party most popular in an area was generally the one most generous with rice and fish heads. What stake could they have in this filthy war?

Yet strangely, the villagers loved to watch the war! During every attack, every troop movement, the natives would run out onto the road, line up, and watch—oblivious, even after all these many years, to the fact they were very much in danger. Especially since the North Vietnamese, knowing the Air Force reluctance to bomb the villages, would dig in their heavy artillery and ack-ack guns in the center of their little hamlets.

So far these particular villages had been spared—thanks to the sharpshooting accuracy of the FAC's phosphorous rocket markers that had pointed out strictly military targets for attack. But if the Air Force had to go after the antiaircraft batteries in the villages... he shuddered. He wanted to see no more death. Particularly of civilians. The sight of the strafed soldiers on the highway had

57

sickened him. And he couldn't shake the vision of the three men who had entered the mine field to search for him. They had looked not much older than boys. They had displayed a lot of guts walking into the mined area. And now one had spilled his to a land mine, and another would go through life with one leg. He felt his stomach churning. Think of something else.

The sun was going down in a blaze of glory, splashing psychedelic colors across the horizon. An Arizona sunset transplanted. He almost exclaimed aloud as the hues lit up the surrounding hills. It would make a beautiful painting to hang in his den. That was a good idea. He would close his eyes and capture those colors, then when he got home he would paint them from memory. He had often thought of taking up painting. Now that he would soon be retiring he would have the time. Let's see, there are golds, yellows, brilliant oranges...

"That's a beautiful painting, Gene."

He looked up. He was only mildly surprised to see Gwen bending over him, right next to his easel. She was wearing her red pantsuit, a favorite of his. "Needs work. Haven't got the colors quite right."

"I like it. The reds and the yellows. We'll hang it in the living room. It will go well with the colors in there. We'll get a nice frame. It will be attractive."

She moved toward him...

He snapped his eyelids open. Good God! His palms were moist. Had he been dreaming or hallucinating? It was all so real! Gwen was actually there, real as life. He had even come to with his lips pursed, ready to give her a kiss.

He shook his head. Cool it. Pull yourself together. He licked his parched lips. It must be the thirst that was doing it. The god-awful thirst. Without water men did crazy things. Thought crazy thoughts...

In the distance, at the edge of the forest beyond the villages, some kind of unintelligible activity was in progress. Hambleton rubbed his bleary eyes and squinted through the haze of late-afternoon sunlight. He could just make out tiny uniformed figures milling about what appeared to be several Russian ZIL two-and-a-half-ton cargo trucks hooked up to some odd-looking trailers. But the distance, the shimmering dust-laden air, and the lengthening shadows combined to frustrate his efforts to interpret the scene.

Then, from the center of the group of men and trucks, a dark slender shape began slowly to rise up toward the sky. As its angle from the shadowy ground increased, its needlelike tip caught a slanting shaft of sunlight. Hambleton's heart sank. Now he understood, all too well.

The thing he was looking at, edged by the gold of the dying sun, was the finned warhead of a SAM-2!

So that was that. Charley had raised the ante all the way. Now the friendly aircraft on which Hambleton was so totally dependent—the FACs, the fighter-bombers, the rescue choppers—would not only have to fly through the fire storms thrown up by conventional antiaircraft cannon and automatic weapons, they would also have to face the deadliest threat to aircraft in the whole theater of operations—the very weapon that had shot his own plane down. Evidently tired of having the Air Force strike from the skies with impunity—strafing their convoys, dropping mines, and generally raising hell—the Communists were going to do something about it. It was also evident that the gomers were more determined than ever to get him before the Americans did.

The target-seeking missiles were far more effective at shooting down aircraft than the antiaircraft guns that ringed the area. Once a target was locked onto the SAM's sophisticated tracking system, it required drastic evasion maneuvers to outwit the homing missiles. It could be deadly if a plane's pilot was unaware that he was a locked-on target, and in any circumstances, it was a murderous threat to slow-moving helicopters. Hambleton knew from his last intelligence briefing that there had been no SAM sites reported in this specific area. The pilots would not be expecting them. They could be knocked off like fish in a rain barrel. He had to do something about it.

He checked in with Birddog, apprising him of what was going on in short, cryptic messages. Birddog acknowledged, surprised that the sophisticated Communist launching systems had been set up so quickly in the move south.

"Got an idea," said Hambleton. "Have all the birds flying in this area tonight monitor Guard channel. I'll play Joe Namath."

"Wilco, quarterback. Birddog out."

Hambleton sat up on the edge of his hole, watching the village and the surrounding woods. In the failing light he could see the finned warheads of several more SAMs pointing up toward the darkening sky. He wouldn't be getting much sleep tonight. As each first-stage booster ignited he would be whispering into his radio, "SAM! SAM! Vicinity DMZ!" Then Birddog would pick it up and rebroadcast the message to all the planes in the area, alerting them in time to take evasive action.

From his experience with SAM firing patterns during his seven months of combat flying, Hambleton figured the North Vietnamese would shoot one or two and that would be the show for the evening. But on this night it was a whole new ball game. They kept sending up missiles steadily for over two hours. He couldn't believe it. After the first few he began counting as he gave the firing warnings to Birddog. After twenty-five launches he lost track.

It was not until heavy clouds rolled in from the sea, all but obscuring Hambleton's view of the launching site, that the missilemen finally hung it up for the night. When it was obvious the firings were over, Birddog checked in. "Nice show, Bat. Either your warnings helped or the gooks are slipping. We didn't lose a bird to the SAMs, and tonight they were thicker'n fleas on a hound dog's butt."

Hambleton smiled grimly. "Good news."

"Call it a night. We'll be coming in tomorrow morning as soon as the ground fog lifts. Need anything?"

"Getting low on cherries for the Manhattans."

"I'll make a stop at the deli. Birddog out."

Hambleton crawled into his hole, reached into his larder, and produced an ear of corn. He ate it ravenously, cob and all. Now if only he had a drink.

As if generated in the thought, a drop of water splashed on his face.

He stifled a war whoop. RAIN! *Bring 'er down, David!* He whipped out his rubber map, spread it out on a bush, then foraged for his plastic water container. It wasn't just sprinkling now, it was coming down in buckets. A squall had whipped the heavy, humid air into a snarling black cloud that was lighting the heavens with its electricity. The rain came down as if a giant hand had pulled the plug in the sky.

Glory be to God! His prayers had been answered. Quickly he scurried around, putting Chester's house into his hole, then covering his lair with branches and fronds to keep it and his survival gear as dry as possible. Then he attended his rain collector.

The map was filling and funneling its contents into the plastic water bottle. In a matter of minutes he was soaked to the skin, but he could hardly have cared less. He raised his face to the sky, mouth open, and let the delicious rainwater run in. He stripped off his flying suit, then his shorts, shoes, and socks. Like a man possessed he hopped around, letting the clean water cascade down his filthy body.

He started laughing uncontrollably. It was raining and he was wet and he would have fresh water to drink again. He wrung out his flying suit, shorts, and socks and hung them over a bush to collect more water, then he wrung them out again and again.

Finally, as quickly as it had appeared, the grumbling cloud gathered up its wet skirts and moved on to the east.

Hambleton checked his container. It was more than half full. Two and a half quarts of good, clean drinking water. He put the jug to his mouth and took huge, ravenous gulps, until he forced himself to stop. This liquid treasure might have to last him longer than he cared to think about.

As a light breeze carried the lingering scud away, he draped his flying suit over a bush to dry. He removed the leaves and branches and jaybird naked, crawled back into his den.

He felt better than he had in a long while. The stubble on his face didn't itch any more. The air smelled good and fresh and clean. Even *he* smelled good. Food in his stomach and now fresh water, a bath for the first time in days, clean clothes, and tomorrow morning—rescue. By God, he *was* going to lick this thing. His survival-school instructors were going to be proud of him. Hell, he might even go on the road as a guest lecturer.

He pulled out Chester's house, and while the furry worm tickled its way across his bare stomach, he replaced the cage's floor with clean, fresh leaves. "If there's anything I can't stand," he murmured to Chester, "it's a dirty housekeeper."

The Fifth Day

In the Pentagon the Chairman of the Joint Chiefs of Staff leaned forward in his swivel chair and studied the face of the colonel who was giving the intelligence briefing.

The Army colonel was glib, articulate, and had polished his performance to a high gloss. When the events of the Asian War during the last twenty-four hours had been covered, and questions from the assembled military chiefs had been answered, the colonel paused, cupped his hands over his pointer, and waited to be dismissed. But the chairman was not quite ready to dismiss him.

"I don't understand," said Admiral Moorer, "why it has taken so long to rescue Hambleton. It's going on five days." He turned to the Air Force Chief of Staff. "John, what the hell's wrong with our SAR?"

Air Force General John Ryan met his eyes. "Admiral, the trouble isn't with our search and rescue units. There are complicating factors. Foremost, as you know, has been the weather. The monsoon season has created low-visibility ground fog that has seriously hampered our Jolly Green rescue attempts. Secondly, Hambleton is in a very hot sector; right now, one of the hottest in Vietnam. He's holed up near the juncture of a main arterial highway bringing in supplies from the north, and the enemy has been able to repulse our choppers every time they were able to get airborne."

"I understand all that. But I also know we've got to get that man out of there. Along with Lieutenant Clark. What the hell are we doing about it?"

"We're going to keep trying, Admiral. We have a mission

scheduled to pick up both the men as soon as the ground fog lifts this morning, Vietnam time. The weather is forecast to be good."

Moorer digested this. "What's the latest on his physical condition?"

"He appears to be in comparatively good shape," said Ryan. "It rained last night. He should have fresh water."

"That's good." The admiral stroked his chin and leaned back in his chair. "What a crazy setup. Here we've got a navigator with a headful of secrets shot down in the middle of an offensive, calling out targets for the fighters and broadcasting SAM alerts. Now that's pretty weird, even for this war."

"Wars don't usually make much sense, Admiral, especially this one," said Ryan.

"No. But every time I think of that fifty-three-year-old navigator dug into the mud out there, I think there must be some hope. It's as if he were trying to win the war all by himself."

"I guess," said the Air Force Chief of Staff, "Hambleton thinks it's important."

Hambleton awoke from four hours of the best sleep he had had since being shot down. He had been dreaming of a squadron clambake he and Gwen had attended during a golf outing....the clams and lobsters steaming from the pots, dipped in melted butter ...the flagons of cold beer...

He wiped melted butter from his lips and stirred himself. It was beginning to turn light. Ground fog licked the terrain, touching everything with moist fingers. Over to the east he could hear the voices of the villagers preparing for a new day. He would give anything to be able to understand their language. The odor of their cooking began to drift his way, reminding him of his dream.

Never mind. Today was the day of his deliverance. As soon as the fog burned off he was going to be taken away from all this. To the land of juicy steaks and eggs and cold beer. And cigarettes. Man, would a cigarette go great! Briefly he wondered how dried cornsilk wrapped in corn husks would burn. Behind the barn in Illinois he had once smoked grapevine.

Forget it! He'd soon be having a Marlboro.

He put a few more leaves into Chester's cage, then crawled out of his hole. Having forgotten his nudity, he was shocked to look down and see the incongruous picture of himself stark naked, except for his veil of mosquito netting. He grinned. Like a bride at a nudist wedding. Well, not exactly a bride. Crawling around on all fours, he gathered up his laundry. It was damp, but it smelled a lot better. He took the clothes back to his hole. It was when he was starting to slip into his shorts that he noticed the marks on his body.

Peculiar. It was the first time he had been out of his flying suit, and he hadn't seen them before. He had been suffering some discomfort, but he had chalked it up to the stiffness of inactivity and sleeping on the damp ground. There were little black spots scattered over his body, mostly concentrated on his right leg and side. Some seemed to be infected. He investigated one on his right bicep. He squeezed it, and to his surprise out popped a little piece of metal.

So that was it. Flak. Picked up when the SAM missile had exploded on impact with his plane. Tiny pieces of pot metal. The Commies and their damned cheap pot-metal missiles. No goddamn class! He spent the better part of an hour squeezing the small sores, removing the pieces of shrapnel, and dressing them with disinfectant. After patching all the festers he could reach, he donned his shorts and flying suit. Then he put on his socks and shoes.

OK. He was ready. He even smelled presentable. The thick fog was being reduced to a thin wisp by the rays of the early morning sun. The weather forecasters were right. It wouldn't be long now until the visibility was CFB (clear as a frapping bell) and the Jolly Greens would be clattering in.

He would probably have time for a bite to eat. He produced his last ear of corn, broke it in half, rewrapped one half in its husks and began eating the other half, chasing it down with gulps from his jug. Ah, nothing like starting the day off with a good breakfast.

As he slowly munched the cob, he could hear the activity of planes to the south and the booming of bombs and antiaircraft guns in the distance. With the big enemy push on, the war seemed to be moving to the south. He knew of a highway bridge that crossed the Song Cam Lo River several clicks to the southwest. This was probably the target his buddies were concentrating on, trying to slow up the rapid advance of the Communists.

The action had also brought out the curious war watchers from the villages. They lined the roads, chattering, pointing at the planes barely visible in the distance, shouting in their high-pitched voices as the bombs fell. Nothing, Hambleton thought, like putting on a little show for the folks. Beats the hell out of television.

Several hours into daylight the fog had completely dissipated. Some of the big guns had been silenced by the attacking fighters, but still Birddog had made no mention of the Jolly Greens. Hambleton hadn't mentioned them either, for he knew the Air Force had its hands full. Besides trying to stem one of the biggest attacks of the war, they now had two downed airmen they had to retrieve. Troubles enough without having to listen to nagging from a guy in a hole.

By monitoring the Birddog's transmissions he knew that Lieutenant Mark Clark was about four miles east of him, being worked by another FAC plane. At one point he had mustered the courage to break radio silence and call Clark direct, but the VHF line-of-sight survival radio had been unable to pick him up. He had only wanted to give Clark a few words of encouragement.

Sitting in his hole waiting and trying to keep his nerves steady, Hambleton tried to keep busy. He spent some time with Chester, letting him romp around on his knee while he mended his cage. But this didn't take long. After berating the worm for being such a wretched housekeeper and replenishing its larder with fresh leaves, he had no choice but to sit back and wait for the call from Birddog.

Strange, he mused, how one's emotions were tied to a yo-yo string in a situation like this. At times his morale was lower than a snake's belly, at other times almost dangerously euphoric. Like this morning. He had started out the day feeling downright cocky. But now, as the morning was turning into noon, with still no word from his FAC pilot, his spirits were beginning to plummet.

After all, he had gone through enough to make a confirmed pessimist out of Pollyanna. In his five days he had seen nothing but a glimpse of a rescue chopper. He had heard them trying to come in, but as far as getting close, let alone land—it hadn't happened. There was no need to kid himself. It was wise to face reality. Some of the antiaircraft guns were well hidden, buried so deep it would take a sewer rat to find them.

If the Jolly Greens couldn't get in, would he be smart to find a way out on his own? Try walking out? Even if he could get through the mine field, would it be possible to get past all those people who had been searching for him every night, undoubtedly monitoring his every move? There was a slim but possible chance. It was even within the realm of possibility that some of the villagers might help him. No, scrub that thought. With the price on his head, he would be too valuable a property to hoard.

He had spent hours studying his map and considering the possibilities of escape in every direction. If he went west he would have to travel some ninety miles to the Laotian border. Then he would have to cross the Mekong River—tantamount, in his condition, to crossing the Gulf of Mexico. And no telling what he'd find on the opposite bank.

By going south he would eventually meet friendly people, providing he could pass through the vanguard of the enemy soldiers pushing south. With his luck he would probably end up in the front lines all the way to Saigon. That thought brought back an old memory of a childhood incident. He and an ornery cousin were digging in the backyard, having decided to dig their way to China. Suddenly his cousin threw down his spoon and proclaimed, "This is a lousy idea. I ain't diggin' through hell just to get to China." Hambleton felt the same way about going south.

Of course, traveling to the north was out. That way lay the Hanoi Hilton.

The only remaining possibility would be to go east, toward the sea. But even that direction was uncertain. He would still be behind enemy lines and there was no way of knowing what he'd find if and when he reached the coast. Any way you sliced it, there was no direction he could go that looked very appealing.

And so the alternative was...eat your corn, pray a lot, keep your mind occupied with positive thoughts, achieve a small goal each day, and leave the rescuing to the Air Force. They knew exactly where he was, his physical condition, and that he had all his faculties. Well, most of them, anyway. So he would just use these faculties, wait patiently, and let the lads do their job. He wasn't going to make it any tougher for them by hiking off across country and playing hide and seek with both the enemy and the best friends he had.

All eminently reasonable, but by noon his spirits had nevertheless reached a kind of nadir. No sign of the choppers; no word from Birddog; couldn't even reach him on the radio. The weather was beautiful, the whole area was quiet. What the hell could the problem be this time?

He tried to think of plausible explanations. Another plane shot down, perhaps. Or bad weather at the base. But he couldn't prevent the unspeakable thought from materializing in his brain.

Dear God, had he been abandoned?

In the briefing room of the Air Force command post, Colonel Walker faced the flying crews seated before him. The men were in sweat-stained flying clothes. Fatigue showed in their faces. Walker's voice was low.

"Okay, gentlemen, that's the briefing. Just one more thing. I know you've been flying your butts off ever since the invasion started. We've set some kind of record for planes downed during this past week, and you've done a hell of a job. But remember, especially you Jolly Greens, the place is crawling with unfriendlies. Throwing up everything from ack-ack to sake bottles. So watch yourselves. Any questions?"

There were none.

"OK. As briefed, Captain Clark will execute his brainstorm plan and give you the word if it's safe enough to go in. Good luck, gentlemen." The crews gathered their gear and started filing out the door. "Oh, Captain Clark."

The Birddog pilot turned to face the colonel. "Sir?"

"I want to talk to you."

"Roger."

After all the crew members had filed out of the briefing room, Walker stuck his face close to Clark's. "When was the last time you had a good night's sleep?"

"Sir, I told you. I'm getting my rest."

"Like hell you are. I'm going to let you take this one mission. Hopefully it will be the last. Then I'm confining you to quarters for twelve hours."

"But, sir, I'm on leave. It's not Air Force policy for a commander to dictate what a—"

"It is not Air Force policy for a smart-assed captain to lip off to a superior officer."

"No, sir."

Walker studied the tired pilot. "Do you know Hambleton?"

"We've talked, sir."

"I mean personally?"

"Never met him, sir."

"Interesting. Would you mind telling me why you want to stay on this mission? You've received your PCS orders! Why are you volunteering? You know as well as I do that someone else can take over."

Clark shrugged. "Everybody seems to be trying to make it into a big thing, Colonel. Like I was some kinda nut. I'm not. I don't know, maybe it's because I spend a lot of time behind the enemy lines and know what it's like out there. Maybe it's because I've been in on several rescue missions, know the ropes, and get a kick when we pull someone out. Don't ask me to explain. All I know is there's a fifty-three–year–old man down there and he's hanging in like a tiger. And maybe I just sort of put myself in his shoes and hope someone would do the same for me. Hell, I don't know. I just want to stay on and see it through. Ain't no big thing."

Walker grunted. "Clark, I don't know whether to put you in for an Air Medal or a psychiatric discharge. Maybe you deserve both. While I think it over, get your butt out of here."

"Yes, sir." Clark started for the door.

Walker called after him. "On this mission. Be careful, Denny."

The revving of the Birddog's engines brought Hambleton scrambling up out of his hole. He flipped on his radio.

"How goes it, Bat Twenty-one?"

"One of those dog days, Birddog. Quiet."

"We're gonna liven it up a little. I'm dropping a CARE package."

Hambleton looked in disbelief at his radio. A CARE package! What the hell for? He was supposed to be getting out of there. "You did say a CARE package?"

"Rog. Sustain your spirits 'til Jolly Greens get in. Stand by. Birddog out."

For Christ's sake! What the hell was going on? This must mean another delay. What the bloody—oh, hell, at least a CARE package would have food in it. Some of it palatable. And water. And cigarettes. And fresh radio batteries...

He heard the buzzing of the little FAC plane. It came in low and slow, flying directly toward his position. As it neared, he could see the plane's door open, then a canister came tumbling out. Its chute barely opened before it hit the ground.

Hambleton swore. The canister had landed on the enemy's side of the Maginot Line.

Immediately Birddog came on. "How was the drop, Bat?"

Hambleton watched as several soldiers headed for the canister. "Piss poor."

"No matter. It was a dummy."

"A *what?*"

"Explain later. Was there much ground fire when I flew over? Any big stuff?"

"Didn't see any. Some small-arms stuff."

"Outstanding. Stand by. Birddog listening out."

Hambleton shook his head numbly. Was he crazy, or were they?

"Birddog to Bat Twenty-one. Come in."

"Bat listening, Birddog."

"Roger. Get ready to pop smoke. Jolly Greens on the way."

Hambleton's heart leaped into his throat. He couldn't believe his ears. "Say again, Birddog."

"Jolly Greens are coming in. Prepare to pop smoke."

Glory be to God! It *was* true! They're coming. *They're finally coming!* he sprang into action, checking his flares, gathering the belongings he was going to take.

Then, as he did so, the pieces began fitting together in his mind. Of course! Those crazy characters had reasons. They wanted to make the gomers think they were abandoning plans to pick him up. By dropping supplies ostensibly to tide him over they hoped to put the enemy off his guard when the Jolly Greens came in. And to top that the Birddog plane had served as a decoy to see how hot the area was. That Birddog pilot! That crazy son of a bitch had actually flown as low and slow as possible over the enemy camp, trolling for antiaircraft fire, testing to see if it were safe enough to bring in the Jolly Greens. If that didn't take the rag off the bush!

Thank God the little plane had only drawn a smattering of small-arms fire. The SAR unit probably figured the accompanying gunship chopper could handle that. Thus they had made the decision to come in. Hot damn! He was gonna run up one helluva bar bill repaying all his debts.

For a moment he debated about taking Chester. Strange, the affinity he had developed with the insect. But it wouldn't be right to take him along, to take him away from his home, out of his environment. Besides, there was a good chance of his getting squashed during the pickup. Anyway, Chester would soon be getting his wings too, and would be taking off on his own.

He reached over, opened the tiny enclosure, and gently removed the furry worm from its nest. As it crawled along his palm he felt a ridiculous sense of sadness. He was saying good-bye to a friend. In the order of living things, few could be much lower than the worm he held in his hand. But it had been a friend. The two of them had been through dark hours together.

Gently he picked up the insect and placed it back into its house, leaving the roof off. He plucked several tender leaves from a bush and put them in with the caterpillar.

"So long, Chester," he whispered. *"Vaya con Dios."*

He heard the unmistakable *chuff-chuff* of chopper rotors. And then he could see them. Two tiny flyspecks in the east. Coming fast. A rescue chopper and its escort gunship.

Birddog came on the air. "Do you have the Jolly Greens in sight, Bat Twenty-one?"

"Affirmative, Birddog."

"Outstanding. QSY to Guard channel. You'll be able to monitor the Jolly Greens as well as myself."

"Roger." Hambleton switched his radio to the common frequency. "Bat Twenty-one testing on Guard."

A deep, businesslike voice came booming in. "Roger, Bat Twenty-one. Jolly Green here. Reading you five square. How me, over?"

"Five by five," answered Hambleton.

"Roger. Will be coming over your spot on a northerly heading. Can you make it to the clearing just east of your position?"

"You better believe it."

"Good. Will effect pickup thirty yards due east your position. Pop smoke and start toward us as soon as we hover into position."

"Wilco, Jolly Green."

Great news! The rescue chopper was going to come in and squat. Hambleton hadn't been all that excited about being winched into a hovering chopper. A winch pickup could take longer, meaning more exposure to enemy fire. He grabbed up his flares, ready to ignite the first one.

Hambleton watched the helicopters fly toward the river. On reaching it they turned north in a diversionary maneuver. Then they suddenly swung directly toward his position, coming in low at full throttle, the prop wash from their rotors leaving a trail of broiling dust.

Hambleton ripped off the flare's striker, poised for his dash to the clearing. Closer and closer they came. Sporadic gunfire started opening up from nearby positions. He could see the flash of machine guns and the trail of smoke from the gunship in the lead, paving the way for the rescue chopper behind, answering fire with fire.

Suddenly his radio crackled. It was the urgent voice of the Birddog pilot. "Jolly Green! Jolly Green! Turn left! Big gun activity in the village twelve o'clock to you. Turn left!" The urgent voice suddenly switched to a yell of anguish. "Left, goddamn it, Jolly Green! LEFT! STAY AWAY FROM THAT VILLAGE! IT'S HOT!"

Hambleton, transfixed, watched as the choppers started to break in a sharp bank away from the village. And then, before his horrified eyes, the reserve chopper was suddenly replaced by a blinding ball of fire. A delayed boom of the antiaircraft gun banged his eardrums.

"*Oh, no!*" Hambleton shook his head in unbelieving horror. "*Oh, sweet Jesus, NO!*"

"Jolly Green's hit!" yelled the Birddog pilot. "Going down... going down..."

Hambleton stared, muted by fear, watching as the chopper dropped from view, leaving a mushroom of smoke in the sky. He felt as well as heard the explosion as it plummeted into the village. His empty stomach retched as he watched the accompanying helicopter turn, and with wheeling, evasive maneuvers hightail it back across the river.

The shocking silence that followed was broken by the leaden voice from Birddog. "Bat Twenty-one, we'll have to back off."

"Understand." Hambleton could barely manage the word as he stared in disbelief at the funeral pyre rising from the village.

He sank back into his hole, indescribable misery and abandonment written on his face. "Whole crew...wiped out," he whispered. "Five men...trying to save me." He sagged, hopelessly. "Five men... five men..."

The Sixth Day

It was thirty minutes past midnight. In the command post of the Korat Royal Thai Air Base several officers were engaged in a heated session with Colonel Walker. A red-eyed, angry Captain Clark was popping off. "Goddamnit, Colonel—"

"Cool it, Captain," snapped Walker. "Just cool it. For the last time. I didn't say we're going to abandon Hambleton. You're punch-drunk tired."

Clark eased off a little. "I thought you said, sir—"

Walker leaned into the young officer. "I said it's got to *look* like we've abandoned him. There's a big difference. Is that clear?"

"No, sir."

Exasperated, Walker looked around the group. "One more time. The enemy is going to keep it hot in Hambleton's sector as long as they know he's alive. Now, you agree with that, Clark?"

"It appears so. Especially after today's—" he checked his watch, "yesterday's mission."

"Especially after yesterday's mission, we can't go in again with choppers as long as they keep it so hot. Agreed?"

"Not necessarily, sir—"

"Believe me. Necessarily. Therefore, the wing staff has come up with a new wrinkle. I'm about to brief you on it, if you give me the chance. It may or may not work. But headquarters thinks it's worth a try. Now if it's all right with you I'll get on with it."

Clark relaxed, looking a little sheepish. "Sorry, sir. I misunderstood. When you said abandonment I thought—"

"I know what you thought. Believe it or not, Clark, the Air Force is just as eager to get back that man as you are. Now as soon

73

as you're briefed, go out and tuck Hambleton in for the night. And don't mention anything to him about this plan. It's top secret. For reasons you'll understand, we don't want to risk any chance of the Charleys getting onto this one."

"Yes, sir."

"And then I want you to report back to your BOQ. And stay there for at least eight hours. And that's an order!"

"Yes, sir."

"Now here's the plan."

Hambleton glanced at his watch. According to the luminous dial it was nearly two A.M. And still sleep had not been able to overpower the thoughts churning in his brain. No matter what he did, he could not erase the image of that black cloud of pulverized metal hanging in the sky; nor could he blot out those words from Birddog. They kept echoing in his brain.

He tried to rationalize the whole unbelievable scene. He knew he should not feel any guilt. Those men were merely doing the job they had been trained to do. Like policemen or firemen, the SAR Jolly Green crews accepted the chances they were taking when they signed on for the job. They had the best training in the world. They were a dedicated gang of men who understood that what they did bolstered the morale of everyone connected with the Air Force. Throughout their history they had never been known to shy away from danger or give up on a downed airman as long as he was alive. Even what had happened today would not stop them. They would be back, one way—some way—or another. And they'd do it again and again as long as it took to finish the job. No regrets, Hambleton. What's done is done.

Yet, goddamnit! If it wasn't for him, five gallant guys would not have been scythed down in the prime of life. Five men paying the supreme price for one. Five men who...

Hold it, get off it, Hambone! Thinking like that won't help anyone. Knock it off. Dwell on something else. Like sex. Or do something constructive. You can't let this gnaw at your innards. Now stir it!

He was about to do something—exactly what, he wasn't sure—when he heard Birddog jazzing overhead. The noise surprised him. It had been so unusually quiet.

"Come in, Birddog. Bat Twenty-one here."

"Roger, Bat. Got some bad news. You'll have no baby-sitter tonight. Anything you need?"

Hambleton stared mutely at his radio. No baby-sitter tonight? What was this all about? It would be the first full night he'd been completely alone. He tried to cover up his dejection with a levity he didn't feel. "Wish you'd call the newspaper. Paper boy didn't show again this morning. How in hell can I keep up with Peanuts?"

"Will check on it, Bat. Just remember. Whatever happens, keep the faith. Birddog out. *Adiós.*"

"*Adiós.*" Ham clicked off his radio, deep in thought. *Adiós.* Was he truly being abandoned? Had the Air Force finally decided it was ridiculous to risk more lives to save one? They would be correct if they did. Somewhere they had to draw the line.

He looked up at the clear sky. Since he had been in his hole he had watched the new moon turn into nearly a quarter. He shut his eyes. And then in spite of his best efforts, he felt the warmth of tears on his cheeks.

Captain Dennis Clark tried to be quiet as he entered his BOQ room so he wouldn't wake his roommate. Not that he was overly concerned about Jake Campbell getting his sleep. He was just anxious to prevent any unnecessary conversation. He was bone tired, and since he had to stand down flying activities for the rest of the night, and since he had been ordered to the sack by the wing commander, he intended to make the best of it.

To hell with the shower. He'd take it in the morning. As he skinned out of his flying suit and slid between his sheets, the bed lamp of his roommate snapped on. A sleepy voice intoned, "That you, Denny?"

"Who the hell did you think it was?"

"Dunno. Didn't think you lived here anymore. How come you ain't flying?" He looked at his watch. "Hell, it's only three in the morning."

"All the local birds are grounded for the next eight hours."

"Oh?" Campbell reached for a cigarette. "What's the deal?"

"Classified. Top secret. Tell you about it later. Go to sleep."

"Heard about the Jolly Green crew getting shot down. Real bummer."

"Yeah."

"How's Hambleton taking it?"

"Hangin' in. He's a gutsy old bastard."

"Too bad they couldn't yank him out. Tonight you could have been pinchin' stewardi on that chartered seven oh seven going to the States."

"Yeah. Go to sleep."

"How much longer, pray tell, do you plan to go on acting as if you are indispensable to this conflict here in Southeast Asia?"

"Till we yank Hambleton out of there."

"Way things are going that could mean another tour."

"So be it."

"I've seen fruit bars in this man's air farce, but you, my friend, win the cut-glass flyswatter."

"We've already established that. Go to sleep."

"You look beat, man. Can I get you a cold beer? Warm body? There's a couple of nurses down the hall that just checked in on an air evac. I'll bet they're horny—"

"You can get me one thing. A large hunk of absolute quiet. And a little solitude wouldn't go too bad."

"OK, spoilsport. Something tells me you don't want to chat." Campbell butted his cigarette, turned out his lamp, and crawled back under his sheet. "So something big's brewing. Big enough to ground the local air war. Should I put on my embroidered flak suit?"

"Won't be necessary. But I sure as hell wish I had one for Hambleton."

"Oh? Why, pray tell?"

"Because in about one hour that poor devil is going to go through Armaggedon and Custer's last stand, all rolled into one."

Hambleton flopped into his hole, his heart beating like a trip-hammer in his chest. This was it. No matter what, he was *not* going to risk another foraging trip to the garden.

At best it was a hairy trip. This time, it had been hairy as an ape. Just after picking several ears of corn, he had had the daylights scared out of him. A Vietcong patrol with flashlights had stopped not far from where he lay hidden in the cornfield. At least a dozen in the patrol, the soldiers had squatted on their haunches and lit up cigarettes as they chatted, the red tips of their smokes glowing brightly as they drew on them.

He had lain deathly still in the furrow, watching their faces leap into bright relief like Halloween masks as one by one they took a last drag, crushed their butts with the heels of their boots, and moved on cautiously. They had checked bushes, scouted the ditches. He had stayed prostrate, frozen, for half an hour. Thank God for that band of gravel. The land mines had prevented them from coming his way. But even when they had gone, it had been a struggle to muster the strength and courage to beat it back to his hole.

Never again. Not even if his stomach started gnawing on his backbone. But now at least he had several ears of corn to sustain him. He removed them from the pockets of his flight suit and started to shuck one, trying to force himself not to think. But as he bit into the sweet kernels he could not help doing it.

Birddog had not been kidding. Hambleton had tried to call just before going to the garden, and there had been no answer. And now it was so quiet it was eerie. Generally there was the sound of aircraft somewhere in the distance, even if it were just his Birddog, or "Blue Chip," the C-130 Airborne Command Post that was always on station directing the air war from on high.

But tonight—nothing. Absolutely nothing. It was Twilight Zone. So vacuum-still he could hear the breath rattling in his lungs. What the hell was going on?

Wait a minute. There's a noise. He quit chewing to listen. It was a strange, far-off, indefinable discord. A sound he had not heard since he'd been out in this hole. He felt that in his environment he had developed his hearing sense to a fine pitch, relying on it so often when his other senses had been thwarted. Now he tried to tune in the noise, bring it into focus. It was getting louder.

At first it sounded like a distant freight train. Now it was developing into a sort of rhythmic whump-whump-whump, and it was coming nearer. Fast!

His first instinct was to reach for his radio and call the FAC. Then he remembered: no baby-sitter tonight. The earth was beginning to tremble. And the faraway whump-whump was turning into whump-*whump*-WHUMP!

He rose up out of his hole.

And then he saw it, huge brown-yellow balls of flame, as high explosives detonated. They advanced in a long line, like giant footsteps heading straight for his hole. And then he understood.

"Jesus H. Christ! It's B-52's! *Bombing this place!*" He flopped into his hole. *"What the hell are they doing?"* He slapped his helmet on his head, dug in, and held on.

BAROOOOM! The earthshaking crescendo peaked as a crater opened up several hundred yards south of him, the concusssion all but knocking him out of his hole. *"Son of a bitch!"* he roared. He huddled, his teeth clenched so hard his jaws ached, his eyes squeezed shut, his arms over his head waiting for the bomb that would hit his hole and blast him to smithereens.

But it did not come. The shock waves began to diminish as the giant craters marched off into the distance.

He straightened up, trembling, wiping the dirt from his eyes and wagging his jaw open and shut to relieve the concussion pressure that blocked his ears. He ran his hands over his body. Except for the loud ringing in his ears, he seemed to be OK. He had weathered the ungodly inferno.

Cursing, he started to rise up out of his hole to look around. Then he heard it again. The far off whump-whump coming from a different direction. *"Oh, God!"* His mind spun back like the reel on a high-speed tape recorder. So this was it. This was why Birddog's voice had had the note of finality in it when he said *"Adiós."* That last message was the kiss of death. That was the Air Force's way of saying good-bye.

Were things really deteriorating so badly they had to expend him to bomb troops and equipment coming down from the north? Was this the only way they could stem the invasion? If so, goddamn if he was about to stay put, to play patsy and get splattered all over the landscape! He'd grab his .38 and make a break for it. He was not going to die at the hands of his own comrades. Even if they had forsaken him. He had to make a decision. Either he was going to pack up his automatic and head out at a high lope, or he was going to be a sniveling coward who hid in a hole and...

He made the decision. He threw himself back into his hole and hugged the earth.

Again came the unbearable noise as the explosions came nearer and nearer, this time to the northwest of him. The earth crawled and humped, bucking him around and showering him with debris as another crater opened up barely a thousand yards to the west.

The shock wave knocked his helmet off, sending his glasses skittering sideways on his face. He balled his fists over his ears, stuck his face between his legs and, like some cowpoke grimly trying to hang on, rode the thundering earth. Finally the blasts again marched off into the distance.

Hambleton sat shaking in his hole, trying to regroup his shattered senses. Abandonment was one thing. *But why the hell were they so intent on blowing him to kingdom come?* Slowly his eyes came into focus; the buzzing began to diminish in his ears. He looked around, batting the dust out of his eyes. And then he saw something that made his heart skip a beat.

A limb, blown from a nearby tree, had crashed down beside his hole—right over the spot where he kept Chester's cage. He jumped from his hole and tore at the tree limb. Beneath it was the flattened cage. An irrational dread stole over him as he gently picked up the little house and explored its contents.

Inside he could just make out the flattened, squashed body of the caterpillar.

Then the distant drums commenced again, marching inexorably toward him—this time from a third direction. As the destruction rolled toward him, he stood up and shook his fist at the black sky. *"You bastards! You bloody bastards! You killed my friend! Goddamn you!"*

Then he flung himself into his hole, the incoherent sounds of his voice drowned in the roar and crash of bombs exploding closer and closer.

In the command post briefing room, Colonel Walker and Major Piccard were studying aerial reconnaissance photos of the B-52 raid.

"Look at those bomb craters," said Walker. "You got to hand it to those SAC bombardiers. They stitched those bomb runs around Hambleton as neatly as you'd tat a doily."

"Tat a doily, sir?"

Walker grunted. "I've got enough smart-assed captains around here. I don't need any smart-assed majors."

Piccard wrapped a grin around his pipe stem. "Yes, sir. That's a neat job of doily tatting if I ever saw one."

"Point is, Sam, how does it look? What have the photo interpreters come up with?"

The intelligence officer stoked his pipe. "Among other things we've certainly got a first for the *Guiness Book of World Records*. First time a B-52 raid was ever used as a diversion in an air-rescue attempt. Considering that the mission was twofold—to try to convince the enemy that we've abandoned Hambleton by making a massive air attack in his area and to try to cool things down in a very hot sector—I'd say we almost certainly accomplished at least the second objective.

"These pictures show that we created a hell of a lot of confusion. And we hit several big gun emplacements, destroyed the SAM site, and got some secondaries. Probably ammo dumps." As Piccard talked, Captain Clark walked in, but Piccard continued.

"And we might even have convinced the enemy we've written off Hambleton."

"I don't know if we convinced the enemy we'd given up our rescue attempts," said Clark, "but according to Colonel Hambleton, we sure as hell convinced him."

Walker looked at Clark. "You just talked to him?"

"Not exactly, sir. He did most of the talking. Mentioned several times that we have a peculiar way of trying to rescue old buddies."

"He didn't understand our strategy?"

"I think I finally got through to him. Did the best I could without tipping off the gooks. What really ticked him off was that his caterpillar was killed in the raid."

Walker looked narrowly at the pilot. "His *caterpillar?*"

"Yes. Colonel Ham had developed quite a friendship with Chester. Since the first day."

"Let me get this straight. A caterpillar. In the classic sense. A little furry worm."

"Yes, sir."

Walker looked at Piccard. "Sam, are you thinking what I'm thinking?"

Piccard puffed on his pipe. "You're wondering if the strain is getting to Hambleton? Is he beginning to show signs of mental imbalance? I don't think so. Not necessarily, not simply because he adopted a caterpillar. Remember, a hole in the ground can hardly be considered a normal human habitat. Life suddenly becomes a microcosm. A person can spend a good deal of time studying the minutiae of life that normally he would never even notice. I once debriefed a fighter pilot who had bailed out over an island in the Pacific. Lived there for several months before being rescued. He had made friends with a tarantula. It's not impossible that tarantula might have helped preserve the pilot's sanity."

Walker grunted. "I'm only concerned with Hambleton's well-being. He's got to stay rational if we're to get him out of there. Good God, it's been six days in that hole! It's enough to make any man go off his trolley."

"Last night didn't help matters," added Clark. "You know the hell he must have gone through during that bombardment!"

"I don't even want to think about it," said Walker. "I just want to concentrate on his recovery. We've *got* to get him out of there!" He turned to the photos. "Sam, what's your intelligence estimate? Did we cool things enough to try another chopper rescue?"

Piccard burned another match in his meerschaum. "The B-fifty-twos did a lot of damage, Colonel. But they didn't wipe out all the enemy guns. The North Vietnamese dig in like moles. Since Hambleton's down right smack in their staging area, they can replace the guns almost as fast as we destroy them. And here's another problem." Piccard tapped the photo with his pipe stem. "See these little villages? To the west of Hambleton's position? The photo interpreters have spotted antiaircraft batteries dug in right in the middle of them. According to Hambleton's report, the gun here in this village is the one that knocked down the Jolly Green crew."

"The hell!"

"With all the civilians in the village," continued Piccard, "and the war watchers, as Hambleton calls them, the Communist gun crews think they're pretty safe. They know it's Air Force policy not to go in and slaughter a bunch of civilians. So they sit there fat and happy, surrounded by villagers, and knock off our planes as they come in."

Walker's jaw clenched. "All right, Sam, you've analyzed the problem. Now let's address ourselves to the solution. We can't get Hambleton out of there until we remove the guns. And we can't remove the guns because they're buried in the middle of a flock of civilians. Therefore it seems we have just one solution. Remove the civilians."

"That would seem like a logical approach," said Clark. "But easier said than done."

"Not necessarily," said Walker. He turned to a sergeant sitting at a nearby desk. "Sergeant Galotti, get me Colonel Black on the phone."

The sergeant picked up the phone and started dialing.

"Who is Colonel Black?" asked Clark.

Walker threw the answer over his shoulder as he moved to the phone. "Black is the CO of the Bullshit Bombers."

"Bat Twenty-one from Birddog. Come in, Bat Twenty-one. *Come in!*" Worry contorted Clark's face as he wheeled the little 0-2 around and came in for another pass, jazzing his throttles. It was his third run over the area and still no contact.

Hambleton had always responded immediately to his calls, as if he had been spring loaded to pounce on his radio the second Clark revved his engine. But now there was no answer. Had something gone wrong? Was he sick? Had he been...Clark gunned his engine, sweeping in low, picking up scattered small-arms fire. Except for the stray soldiers taking potshots at him, things appeared fairly quiet in the hazy sunlight below. "Goddamn it, man! Bat Twenty-one, *come in!*"

"Hello, Birddog. Bat Twenty-one still here."

Relief flooded over Clark as he heard the voice from below. "Goddamn, Bat! You scared the bejesus outa me!"

"Sorry, Birddog. I had a priority call from Mother Nature. Ever tried digging a latrine with a hunting knife?"

Clark grinned with relief. "Can't say as I have."

"Ain't easy. I figured if I was going to be around a while I'd add a few conveniences. Also I'm going to start saving my corncobs."

"Outstanding. But we're hoping you won't need 'em. We're coming up with another plan."

"Another one? Hope it's a helluva lot better than the one last night."

"It's quieter. Just hang in while we execute it."

"You execute your plan. In the meantime I'll try to keep from being executed by the gomers. I suppose it's a secret."

"Naturally. Want to keep the gooks on their toes."

"Understand."

"Need anything?"

"Next CARE package, you might include some TP."

"Roger," chuckled Clark. Hambleton was sounding more like himself again. "Birddog listening out."

Hambleton switched off his radio. He was feeling better. His old Birddog buddy had not abandoned him. Nor had the Air Force. They were still in there slugging. He felt like an orphan who had just been repossessed by his family.

He had had lots of time to fill in Birddog's necessarily sketchy reason for the bombardment last night. As nightmarish as it had been, he felt he fathomed it now. It had been a first. He had known of no other time when SAR had used a B-52 raid as a diversionary tactic. B-52's did not come cheap. And whether or not the gomers were convinced the Air Force had given up on him, or squashed him like Chester, things were undoubtedly a hell of a lot quieter.

He brought a piece of corn up from his cellar, stripped it, and started eating. Things were so tranquil he decided to sit up on the edge of his hole and have his snack—look around and get some sun.

He did so, and as he perched on the edge of his hole munching, a movement on the outskirts of the nearest village caught his eye. A cluster of soldiers was gathered around a lone two-and-a-half-ton truck. They were taking something out of it. Curious, he hunkered down and crawled along on his stomach to the edge of the woods. He peeked through the cover, and then his morale plummeted as he recognized the equipment that was being removed from the truck.

Mine detectors!

Now it was just a matter of time before the only barrier between him and the enemy would be wiped out. He groaned. While the Air Force had deftly been dealing the cards, the Commies had quietly been cornering all the aces.

Again the feeling of utter hopelessness surged over him. Gripping his half-eaten cob in his teeth, he crawled back toward his hole to notify Birddog.

Gwen Hambleton looked at her friend. "Marge, I really don't think I should. Something tells me I should be here, near the phone—"

"Nonsense! That's exactly what you need to get away from. You've been sitting by that phone day and night now for nearly a week. You need to get away."

"But what if something should happen? What if they should need to get word to me?"

"Look! Ham's ten thousand miles away. He's got the whole Air Force looking after him. Now just what could you do if he did have a problem?"

Gwen nodded. "You're right. Maybe it would be good for me to get away for a few hours."

"You know it would. Besides," she grinned at Gwen, "I don't have to remind you that you have an obligation to the Davis Monthan Women's Golf Association. The tournament starts next week. If we don't get to Phoenix and pick up those golf trophies we're going to have to face the wrath of thirty women. A fate worse than death."

Gwen returned her friend's smile. "I'll get ready. Be with you in a jiffy. There's iced tea in the fridge."

"I'll find it. Scoot."

Marge was pouring herself a glass of iced tea when the phone rang. It was a man's voice, identifying the caller as being from the Air Force Casualty Center in San Antonio. He asked for Mrs. Hambleton.

"She can't come to the phone just now. This is Marge Wilson, a close friend. May I take a message?"

The man politely agreed. As he talked, the color slowly drained from Marge's face. When the message had been delivered she asked several questions, thanked him, and hung up. Then Gwen came into the room.

"I hope I've got everything. I seem to be about as organized as a Chinese fire...." Her eyes fell on Marge sitting stiffly at the bar, her face ashen. "Marge? What is it?"

"There was a phone call from the casualty center. Honey, you'd better sit down."

"It's not...."

"No, Ham's all right. Ham's all right. They tried to send a rescue helicopter in to pick him up. It was hit. No survivors. But Ham wasn't in it. He's okay."

"Dear God in heaven!"

Gwen collapsed on a barstool as Marge tried to comfort her. "I know this is a terrible shock. But don't let it get to you. The casualty officer said they'll keep trying. They're still in communication with Ham. They'll get him out."

Gwen fumbled into her purse, pulled out a handkerchief. She dabbed at her tears. "I know they will. But right now I'm not thinking of Gene." She looked up at Marge, her face contorted. "I'm thinking of the men in that helicopter…and their families. It's all so horrible!"

It was midafternoon. Dog tired from having been up most of the night, Hambleton had tried to take a nap in the warm sun, but had given up. Every time he was about to nod off there would be another explosion. The soldiers manning the detectors had kept right at their assignment. Every time they detected a land mine they would destroy it. Sleeping had been impossible. He had finally crawled to his vantage point overlooking the paddies, and was now watching the soldiers as they nibbled away at the outside perimeter of his Maginot Line.

From time to time a Sandy would wheel down out of the sun, strafe the area, and—with a howl—disappear back up into the clouds. It was a delaying tactic at best. At the first sound of impending attack, the soldiers would run for cover, then once the plane was gone they would return to their mine-sweeping operation as though nothing had happened. In the course of the afternoon, two more loads of gravel had been dropped. They added to the frustration of the enemy but did little toward solving the long-range problem.

As Hambleton watched, his spirits sinking with every detonation, his ears picked up an unusual sound in the sky. It was different, not the whine of the jets nor the buzzing of the fighters. He finally recognized it as the distinctive drone of turboprop engines. A Hercules C-130?

What was a Specter doing, coming over to strafe with its Gatling guns? The big, cumbersome airplane would make too good a target in broad daylight. To risk it on a strafing run when the faster fighters could handle that more productively made no sense. What then?

Up from behind a low mountain popped the big camouflaged

airplane. Escorted by two Sandys, it came in low, almost treetop level, under the enemy radar and ground-control intercept. Whatever the plane was doing here, it must be part of the plan Birddog had talked about.

Fascinated, Hambleton watched the Hercules swoop over the nearest village, Sandys on each wing tip. There was no sound of gunfire, save for sporadic sniping rifle fire from the soldiers on the ground. Directly over the village a blizzard of white came bursting out of the C-130's cargo hatch. As the plane roared over the other villages the same thing happened, leaving a series of puffy clouds in the sky drifting toward the ground. Completing its last pass before the antiaircraft guns could even be cranked up, the big plane thundered away, hedgehopping over hills to the north and disappearing from sight, the Sandys right at its heels. Not a shot had been fired by any of the planes.

Hambleton scratched his head. What was this all about? What kind of hand was now being dealt in this cockamamy, no-limit game of survival with the North Vietnamese? What had been the purpose of this Bullshit Bomber? Thoughtfully he watched the little clouds float down around the villages.

Hambleton recalled Colonel Black's outfit. In fact he had, on occasion, even bent an elbow with the crusty, eccentric genius who commanded the psychological warfare unit. Colonel Ed Black was a slender, precise man who had the bearing of a trade-school professional. A blizzard of white hair stormed continuously over his scowling eyes, and he talked in the clipped tone of the West Point graduate. Flying AC-130's and U-10's equipped with loudspeakers, his unit dropped propaganda leaflets and broadcast the tapes used in the psy-warfare program.

The Bullshit Bomber unit had been successful. By dropping leaflets printed in the local Vietnamese language over enemy strongholds, the outfit had averaged a VC defection for every hour of flying time it put in. It was, in Black's words, "A pretty inexpensive method of removing nearly two divisions of enemy soldiers from the battlefield." Hambleton had agreed.

Black had shown him a couple of the propaganda leaflets, and had translated them into English. The first was a safe-conduct pass. It guaranteed preferential treatment to any enemy soldier who would turn himself over to South Vietnamese authorities. The other was a simple leaflet stating there was going to be a heavy attack in a certain area, and warning all peasants and civilians in that area to evacuate immediately with their women and children.

"We also promise them a nice hot meal and shelter if they evacuate a battle area," Black had said. "If you can't grab them by the balls, grab them by the stomach. Their hearts and minds will follow. I like my type of war. Very little bloodshed."

"What about the Vietnamese who can't read?"

"We've covered that too. We fly over the area with our speaker planes until time for the attack. Have you ever heard one of our planes?"

God, yes, Hambleton had. You couldn't spend more than a day or so in this theater of war without hearing one of the damned things. It would wake the dead. The taped messages were prepared by the psy-warfare people, and augmented when necessary with live broadcasts from VC who had defected from their local area. It was astonishingly effective.

Now here he was, watching many thousands of messages floating down in a blizzard over the villages. Soon the noncombatants would evacuate. And some of the Communist soldiers might even waver once they knew their positions were no longer immune to attack.

Hot damn! The boys back at the head shed must be preparing for an all-out offensive. With the evacuation of the civilians they could come in over the villages and wipe out the guns once and for all. And then, by God, they could bring the choppers in. Safe and sound. Hallelujah!

Then he sobered. He remembered what else Black had said about his psychological warfare program—the harassment missions. It wasn't going to be quiet.

"Harassment missions are most productive," Black had said. "We often fly them in conjunction with our leaflet drops. Ever heard the tapes of our funeral dirges?"

"No," Hambleton had said.

Black had told him to count his blessings. There was nothing like a Buddhist funeral dirge played at eardrum-splitting intensity. There were also tapes of babies crying; passionate women panting for their husbands and lovers; little one-act skits using professional actors who talked of homesickness and the dangers faced by family separations.

"If nothing else," Black had concluded, "I wager the VC is bushed from being kept awake by the noise all night.

So if things went according to pattern, Hambleton would have another sleepless night. And things seemed to be going according to pattern, for up the Hercules popped again—turboprops biting the humid air—from behind the hills to the north. This time it was alone, the Sandy escorts keeping their vigil from on high lest their drone block out the loudspeaker's message. Even from his position Hambleton almost had to cover his ears as the loudspeakers, kicking out God knows how many decibels, blasted the landscape. The message was in Vietnamese, but Hambleton had no trouble guessing its content. Wailing out in the indigenous dialect, it would be warning all who could not read the leaflets that they should vacate the villages and head south as quickly as possible.

The plane delivered its message, then vacated as quickly as it had come, growling out of sight before any of the big guns had a chance to really lock onto it.

Hambleton assumed the bullshit bombers would be back during the night. Cloaked in the security of darkness they could orbit almost unmolested, blasting out their tapes and their funeral dirges until a man would very nearly be separated from his sanity. But he wouldn't complain. He knew the speaker plane was for his benefit. If it worked, the fighters would be able to come in and destroy the firepower that kept his rescuers at bay.

His eyes returned to the soldiers manning the minesweepers. Except for stopping to take potshots at the low-flying planes, they had barely interrupted their labors. They were making headway. From the looks of things, another twenty-four hours would see the mine field cleared—at least enough to make a passage through. The Sandys would drop more gravel, of course, and keep harassing them. But until the villagers had evacuated, the Air Force could not bring the massive firepower to bear on the villages that was required to destroy the guns. It was going to be a tight race as to who got to him first: the determined Vietcong or the equally determined Air Force. Any way you sliced it, he was getting damned tired of being the pawn in this hellish chess game.

Pawns tended to get eliminated.

The Seventh Day

It had been a wild night. Times Square on New Year's Eve. The Calgary Stampede. The New Orleans Mardi Gras.

The psy-warfare Hercules with its nerve-shattering loudspeakers had not been Hambleton's only company. The BS bomber had a twin sister, far more lethal and eerie. And it was this sibling, known as the AC-130 Specter, that had made a spectacular entrance onto the stage of Hambleton's private war. It was an appearance he had welcomed with open arms. In fact, having once flown a mission in one, he even had developed a sort of kinship with the big, lumbering airplane.

The AC-130 was the latest version of the original "Puff the Magic Dragon" gunship concept. It had replaced the old Gooney Bird C-47, and later the AC-119 Stingers. It was a veritable flying arsenal. Poking out of ports in its capacious belly were rows of machine guns and 20-mm revolving-barreled Gatling guns that could each spit out six thousand rounds per minute with pinpoint accuracy. And it carried plenty of ammunition to keep them going steadily! Other intriguing armaments being tested in the big plane included 40-mm Bofors machine cannon and even a special 105-mm howitzer which had a recoil that all but sent the big aircraft flying sideways.

Last night, watching it all from the ground, Hambleton had been overwhelmed. The fireworks had started after dusk. The enemy, knowing of the impending attack because of the dropped leaflets, had accelerated their efforts to reach him. More mine detectors had been brought in, and there were now half a dozen employed in trying to clear a path through the mine field.

Not to be upstaged, the FAC had brought in Sandys to strafe and drop load after load of gravel. By dusk it had still been a stalemate. Hambleton remained protected, but with the coming of darkness his optimism had started sinking with the sun. Darkness would definitely be on the side of the enemy.

But again, the Air Force had another ace up its sleeve. Thanks to the Hercules gunships, the black curtain of night was seldom lowered. Coming in low under the radar fence, the AC-130's dropped their powerful one-million-candlepower flares, which instantly turned night into high noon. Hidden by the blinding magnesium flares in the sky and flying under the GCI's radar, Specter was virtually invulnerable to the heavy antiaircraft guns. Flying with her lights out, the only way to spot her was in the brief moments she would let loose with her Gatling guns. Then her red tongues of flame flickered down like those of some mammoth dragon, licking out the lives of the men working with the mine detectors.

As the night had progressed, Hambleton began breathing a little easier. The Air Force was more than holding its own. It was keeping the Vietcong at bay in spite of their growing numbers. And now, well past midnight, the soldiers had actually retreated from the perimeter of the mine fields. It was the first time the gomers had actually failed to return with their minesweepers after a strafing attack of the Sandys or the AC-130's.

And then he saw why.

In the next burst of brilliance from the flares he observed the column of refugees.

It was a motley group of old men, women, farmers, children—noncombatants heeding the leaflets dropped by the psy-warfare plane. They were filing out of the villages and heading south. Their belongings were stacked high on oxcarts, A-frames, bicycles, wheelbarrows—anything that could serve as a conveyance. Herded along with them were all manner of livestock, their cackling and mooing and braying adding to the cacophonous din of war.

Hambleton felt a knot growing in his stomach. Nothing like uprooting half a dozen villages and dispossessing whole families so that the game of war could continue. Was he responsibile for this too? If not for him, would these villagers be allowed to stay and work their fields and live their lives in peace under the Communist yoke? Perhaps, but then again ...

Oh hell, Hambone, you don't know! At least the soldiers were letting the villagers leave in peace. But then, as he watched the tragic scene before him, he realized something else.

The refugees were being allowed to leave, all right, but the soldiers had carefully selected their route of departure. The column was being guided right along the outside perimeter of the mine field, as close as possible to where the minesweepers had been working. The reason was clear. This explained the enemy's fallback. The gomers had organized the refugee line of march right through the firefight zone, forcing it close to the land mines. They knew the Air Force would think twice before strafing so close to women and children.

"God a'mighty!" muttered Hambleton. "Those dirty little bastards." He clicked on his radio, checked in with Birddog. He explained the situation.

"Roger, Bat," said Birddog. "The plot thickens. Will have to back off until the refugees are out of there. Keep in touch."

"Roger."

Now it was going to be tough stopping the North Vietnamese, who had now gone back to work on the land mines. Unmindful of the hapless refugee who might be in the way when one of the mines was detected and detonated, the soldiers worked their way inexorably forward, clearing a path. At this rate daylight would find a corridor cleared—and there was not a thing the Air Force could do to stop them. At least not until the last refugee had filed out of the zone.

Hambleton checked his watch. Almost three. A good several hours until daylight. If only the refugees would get the hell out of there! He fought the urge to shout to them, urge them to hurry along. How long would it take to empty the villages? An hour? Several? The attack wasn't scheduled to start until daybreak. So they knew they had time, and they seemed to be in no hurry.

How long would it take for the mines to be cleared enough to make a path through? Several hours? Judging by the increasing frequency of the exploding mines, the gomers were making good time. There was only one comforting thought: The Sandys would be able to come in with more gravel, and not risk killing civilians. With their precise aim they could probably reseed the cleared areas almost as fast as the enemy could sweep them. But all things considered, it was now back to nip and tuck.

Hambleton was damnably tired. Several times he found himself napping with his eyes open as he scouted the scene before him. He had to stay awake. Keep on his toes. Gomers coming closer. Better order more gravel from Birddog. As long as old Specter was up there dropping flares and there was good visibility, the Sandys could spot their target and drop their loads exactly. Have to keep them coming.

Then he saw the thick carpet of gray unrolling toward him, spreading across the paddies. He swore as he watched the early morning ground fog moving in briskly from the east.

There went visibility, and with it the Specters, the Sandys, and the jets. There went protection.

And there went the ball game.

His head fell on his arms. Drugged by lack of sleep, emotionally drained, he could not even think straight anymore. He didn't care what happened. No more. No more playing the Kewpie prize at the carnival. To hell with it.

How much was an old poop expected to take, anyway? Every man had his breaking point. His point had just broken. So they lost the ball game. They had played the game damned hard but they had been defeated. So what? Screw it. Quit fighting the problem.

Painfully, he crawled back to his hole and fell in. Before he could even finish pulling the ground cover over himself, his mind was totally engulfed by the dreamless sleep of utter exhaustion. Even the sporadic detonation of land mines couldn't penetrate it.

"Hey, roomie," said Jake Campbell. "That's a white-knuckle grip on the controls if ever I saw one. I thought you pilots were dashing, carefree, and relaxed."

Clark glanced across the cockpit. "You wanted to come along as observer. Now observe. Dispense with the funny sayings or I'll take you back and drop you at your finance office."

"We're getting a bit testy! Uptight—uptight?"

Clark banked the O-2 over into a split S and screamed for the ground. "I *am* uptight, Jake. Uptight as hell. I will be until I know what's going on under that fogbank down there."

Heading down in a howling dive, Clark buzzed Hambleton's position, or the position as best he could determine it, beneath the thinning layer of fog. He jazzed the throttle, then whipped up into a tight climb.

"Do you have to do that?"

"Do what?"

"Acrobatics. I just swallowed my Adam's apple."

Clark shot him a look of disdain. "Finance officers! What did you expect, a seat at a piano bar?"

"I notice you don't say those nasty things to me on payday."

Clark punched his transmitter button. "Bat Twenty-one. Bat Twenty-one. This is Birddog. Come in, Bat. *Come in!*"

There was no response.

"Jake," said Clark, winging over and slicing off altitude. "I'm worried. Only once before has Hambleton failed to acknowledge. He sleeps with his radio. I'm going down low over the mine fields. Look closely and see if you spot any sign of gooks."

"Must we?"

"We must." Clark dove for the ground, leveling off just as his wheels touched the low-hugging fog. The prop wash sent the wispy vapor to roiling, uncovering parts of the ground.

Looking behind as the plane roared over, Campbell let out a squawk. "I see them! The prop wash ripped the fog away. Got a glimpse of several soldiers."

"Were they working minesweepers?"

"Couldn't tell."

"We'll make another pass." The mist, being rapidly dissipated by the sun and rolled back by the prop blast, lay bare a large section of the mined area. On the second pass the ground was even more discernible.

"Banzai!" yelled Campbell. "I saw them. Working their minesweepers. I guess that's what they were—a long-forked gadget—"

"That's it! Outstanding! That means they haven't gotten through to Hambleton yet. How close to that line of trees were they?"

"Couldn't tell." For the moment, Campbell's discomfiture with the roller coaster ride took a backseat to the thrill of the adventure. "Let's go down again." The plane wheeled over and came down again, and this time it was evident the soldiers were very near the tree line. "See them?" shouted Campbell.

"Roger," said Clark. "The fog must have slowed the gooks up too. Thank God we're not too—"

"Hey, Clark!" A small hole had appeared in the windshield. "Those bastards are shooting at us!"

"Do tell."

"Let's get our asses outta here!"

"We're just starting to work. Get a grip on your hemorrhoids and hang on." Clark rechanneled his radio and clicked his transmitter. "Birddog to Gumshoe. Over."

"Roger, Birddog. Gumshoe here," came back the voice of the Sandy element leader.

"The gooks haven't gotten to Hambleton, not yet. But they're about to. I'm going to paint a target. It's just at the edge of that thinning fog patch. Come in ASAP. Over."

"Roger, Birddog. You mark, we'll bark."

Again Clark rolled over into a steep bank and headed down. He took a bead on the soldiers, barely visible in the wispy condensation, and fired two marking rockets. No sooner had he pulled up in a sharp climb than the Sandys were coming in, their 20-mm cannon chattering. As Clark Immelmanned out of his climb, he could see the soldiers fleeing back toward the village. They were not doing too well. The withering fire from above was lashing them.

Clark wiped the sweat from his forehead with a gloved hand. "That was too goddamn close. Another half hour and the gomers would have been through."

"Jeezus, Clark! *Look out!*"

Clark turned to his roommate, who was pointing wildly out the window. The Sandys, having completed their first strafing pass, had pulled up to wheel over for another run. They passed so close to the banking Birddog that for a split second their flashing image filled the windshield. Hitting their prop wash, the O-2 almost flipped over on its back.

"What's the problem?" asked Clark, righting the airplane.

"Problem! Good Christ, those wild men missed us by inches! What the hell...."

"That's Speedy Gonzales. Element lead. Doesn't think he's made a good strafing pass unless he flies through my antenna. Good man."

"Jeezus, is every mission like this?"

"No. Not all. Sometimes it gets hairy out here."

Clark put his finger to his lips as he turned up the volume on his radio. He spoke into his transmitter. "Bat Twenty-one, that you? This is Birddog. Come in."

Hambleton's sleepy voice came in clear. "Bat Twenty-one here. Birddog. What's all the commotion?"

"Damn, Bat! You're gonna be the death of me. I couldn't raise you."

"Guess I really conked out. Too many parties at night. It caught up with me."

"Understand. We're mending your fence now. Have all the refugees cleared out?"

"Stand by. Will take a look."

Clark turned to his roommate and slapped him on the back. "He's okay. You hear that?"

"I'm delighted. I really am. Wish I could say the same. I think I'm going to be sick."

"No time for that. We're going to make some low passes over the villages. See if you can spot any civilians."

"We gotta go down there again?"

"We do." Clark winged over, poured the coal to the little O-2, and headed for the deck. They skimmed over the villages, one by one hugging the main roads so low they could see into the hooches, their prop wash dusting the thatched roofs.

Except for the soldiers, the villages appeared to be deserted. Not so much as a pig or a chicken was in evidence. After the first pass they drew scattered rifle fire from the soldiers.

Clark pulled up, reaching for altitude. "See anything?"

"My life flashing before me."

"Any refugees? Civilians?"

"No."

"Good. Did you notice the big guns? Dug in that village to the north?"

"No."

"There's also a battery in that old temple."

"Were they shooting at us?"

"Not the big ones. Just the little ones."

"That's mighty comforting. Let's go home."

"Birddog from Bat Twenty-one. Over."

Clark thumbed his transmitter. "Come in, Bat."

"From where I'm sitting I couldn't see any refugees or war watchers. Seems they've all pulled out."

"Affirmative, Bat. We didn't spot any soldiers either."

"Glad to know the gomers have pulled back. According to where they dropped the mine detectors, they got in pretty close. Expected to wake up this morning with my throat cut."

"Too damned close. Fog must have slowed them up. Great duty trying to clear a mine field in the fog. Anyway, the Sandys just put a burr in their tail. With the villages clear we can start bringing in the heavy stuff. See if we can't silence the ack-ack once and for all."

"I'll drink to that."

"Roger, Bat. Stay in the basement. Birddog out." Clark rechanneled his radio and again talked into his mike. "Birddog to all flight leaders. The area is clear of civilians. Anything moves down there it's Charley. No change on assigned targets. Prepare to rally around the flagpole. Heavy stuff first. Bilk Fourteen, you read?"

"Five square, Birddog," came in the leader of the F-4's.

"Roger. State your position."

"In orbit over target at sixteen grand."

"Armament?"

"Twenty-four hundred rounds of twenty mike mike. Forty-eight CBU-fifty-twos."

"CBU-fifty-twos? Outstanding. Only friendly in area is me, orbiting at four grand southwest of target. Use caution. I know you don't care about me, but I got our finance officer aboard."

"Payday's coming up. Tell him he's safe. Bilk Fourteen coming in."

"Roger, Bilk. You got the ball."

Clark fire-walled the throttle to get into position. As he started to climb he noticed his roommate looking at him quizzically. "Got a problem, old-timer?"

Campbell shook his head dumbly. "No problem. I got no problem. Airplane drivers got problems. What the hell you guys got against speaking English? What's going on?"

"You're about to find out. See that village to the east? There. A flash is coming from the center of it."

"I see it."

"That's the gun that shot down the Jolly Green chopper. We're about to put it out of business. Here come the F-fours now."

Campbell watched in awe as the four fighter-bombers came flashing down out of the sun in elements of two, hurtling toward the village in a steep descent. "And there's one thing more that came out of the fighter jock conversation," Clark added as the air war opened up around them. "It was decided that after this mission the finance officer was buying the drinks for all hands."

Campbell met Clark's eyes. "Get me out of this in one piece, roomie, and I'll buy drinks for the whole bloody South Vietnamese Army."

Major General Daniel O'Hearn, the husky, white-haired deputy commander of the Seventh Air Force, was seated in front of the desk of Colonel John Walker. The two officers were studying the latest reconnaissance photos of the morning's mission. Major Sam Piccard looked over their shoulders.

"I'll say this," said O'Hearn, "the boys did one hell of a job on those villages."

"A very successful strike," said Piccard. "Leveled nearly every primary target."

O'Hearn bent closer, peering through the magnifying glass at one of the photos. "These positions you circled on these hills around the village, Major, you're sure they're gun emplacements?"

"Yes, sir. According to our photo experts. As well as those others there in the banana grove just north of the river."

"Why didn't we clobber them on this morning's mission?"

"They weren't listed on the target charts, General. They're brand new. Probably established within the last twenty-four hours."

"How the hell can they get into position like this without our seeing them?"

"It's the fog, sir. Charley loves it. When it socks in they scurry around like moles. Digging in, bringing in replacements faster than we can knock them out."

"From the looks of things we still haven't sanitized the area. In spite of today's all-out operation."

"No, sir. Because of this road here, coming down from the DMZ. They bring supplies down this main arterial from the north in a never-ending stream."

"And we're prohibited from flying north of the DMZ to hit their source of supply. Great way to run a war!"

"Hambleton couldn't have picked a worse spot in the whole Asian theater to chute into," said Walker.

O'Hearn bent low over one of the photos, squinting through the glass. "Major, what's this? Looks like something stacked up here near the wooded area where Hambleton's holed up."

Piccard looked at the spot where the general was pointing. "That, General, is a stack of coffins. Wooden coffins."

O'Hearn looked up at the intelligence officer. "Coffins? A stack that size?"

"Yes, sir. Coffins are a great morale booster to the North Vietnamese. If they think they're going to go to their eternal Kamavachara in a nice new wooden box, they will literally die fighting. And they've already expended quiet a few troops in the operation to get Hambleton."

"From the looks of things they're prepared to expend more. They must want him damned bad."

"I don't know about the North Viets, General," said Piccard, "but their friends the Russians do. As you know, we're spending millions trying to retrieve a Russian missile sub sunk in deep ocean water, just to get the Russian targeting information. I'm sure they have urged their Viet buddies to go for broke to get hold of this live Colonel of ours with SAC targeting information locked in his head."

"The Pentagon confirms that the North Vietnamese probably know who Hambleton is."

"I don't doubt that for a moment, General," said Piccard. "With the help of their Russian friends, I'd be very surprised if they didn't have his complete dossier. They certainly keep tabs on our key officers. Especially those in the SAC missile business."

O'Hearn sighed. "Holy Christ, what a bag of worms!"

Walker leaned back in his chair. "I'm glad you're here, General. It will expedite our coordination with higher headquarters. We've got the Jolly Green crews standing by. Ops orders are being drawn up now. Give the word and we'll go in."

O'Hearn looked up at Walker, then to Piccard. "Major, give me your intelligence estimate. We know there are several guns surrounding Hambleton's position that we can actually see in the reccy photos. Is it not true there could be any number dug in and camouflaged? Guns we couldn't detect in these photos? Guns we've never even targeted? For that matter, guns that could have been brought into position even after these photos were made?"

Piccard puffed on his pipe and shot a look at Walker. "That's true, sir. Especially being so close to the resupply area."

"And the enemy very much wants our downed airman, will go all out to get him, and will try like hell to stop us from getting to him first."

"True, yes, sir."

O'Hearn went on. "Then, gentlemen, I'm afraid we'll have to rule out another Jolly Green rescue attempt.

Colonel Walker blinked. "Dan, did you just say what I thought you said?"

"I'm afraid I did, John. Another rescue attempt by Jolly Green is out."

Walker's eyes narrowed. "Now just a minute. Hambleton's been living in that hole a damned *week*. Very little food or water. And he's no young kid, Dan. He's damned near as old as we are. He's probably near the limit of his endurance. The uncertainty, the constant worry must be gnawing him to death. On top of that we've been raising hell all around him. How much more do you think that man can stand?"

"You don't have to tell me all this, John. We've kept right on top of this thing at headquarters. Not to mention the Pentagon breathing down our necks. One of the reasons I'm here now."

"Then surely you realize that we can't just sit around on our butts and—"

"Now hold on, John. I don't call losing a rescue chopper and launching a B-52 strike exactly sitting around on our butts. For your information, using B-52's to support a rescue mission took one hell of a lot of convincing. General Abrams himself bulled that operation through."

"I appreciate that, sir. But what you don't seem to realize is that one of my men is down. Never in Air Force history have we written off a flyer still breathing behind enemy lines."

"Damnit, we're not writing Hambleton off! But you've got to measure the odds. You're a good commander, John. One of our best. You know we can't let personal feelings dictate what we do."

"All I'm asking is one more rescue attempt. While we've got Charleys reeling from a terrific pounding. They damned near got to Hambleton last night, working in the fog. If the scud hadn't cleared when it did so the Sandys could go in, this whole conversation would be academic. With their mine detectors they're sweeping our gravel faster than we can sow it. Time is running out.

There's a volunteer Jolly Green rescue crew eager to make another try. All we need is your okay. How about it, General?"

"No dice, John."

Walker stared, then slammed his fist down hard on the desk. "But, General ... why? ... *why?*"

O'Hearn rose. "Because yesterday I wrote five sympathy letters to next of kin. How do you justify to five widows or sweethearts that their men traded their lives for a chance to save one man?"

"But that's the name of the game! That's what the air-rescue service is all about. They're hot to trot. Goddamn, General, *that's their mission!*"

"I don't need you to brief me on the air-rescue mission. If this were a normal situation the Jolly Greens would have yanked Hambleton out of there long ago. But this is *not* a normal situation. You're asking rescue choppers to go into one of the hottest areas in Vietnam. You know how vulnerable a chopper is. Hell's fire, you can knock one down with a rock. I've got a mission too, Colonel. And it's to make a very careful assessment of a military situation before commiting men and equipment. I have assessed this situation, and I don't like the odds. I will *not* authorize another rescue mission into that firefight zone. Especially since we've already tried it once and failed."

"And in making your assessment, General, did you crank in the factor that our downed airman is a former SAC staff officer? That the Commies won't give up until they get him? And with their torture they'll crack him like a walnut?"

"I did, yes. I realize we've got to get Hambleton out of there. And fast. But I don't believe authorizing another suicide mission is going to help matters a damn bit. And I sincerely believe, based on our latest intelligence, another suicide mission is exactly what I'd be authorizing."

Walker slumped back in his chair, trying to digest the decision. "Very well, General. I take it that's final."

O'Hearn spoke softly. "That's final, John. I know you think I'm taking a hard line. And I guess I am. I just don't want to needlessly throw away any more lives in this dunghill of a war with its ridiculous ground rules."

"But at least we agree we've got to get Hambleton out," said Walker. "But how? Any ideas?"

"We've got the staff at headquarters working on several ideas. Some of them are pretty far out. I suggest you get your staff together too. Have a brainstorm session."

"Right away. We'll go back to the drawing board. We'll come up with something. We have to."

"I'll also prod the Pentagon. Maybe some of the brain trusters up there can come up with some ideas." O'Hearn rose, moved to the window, and stared out of it. Finally he said, "I know exactly how you feel, John. Believe me, I know."

Walker did not answer. Piccard stoked his meerschaum with a kitchen match, squinted through the smoke, and said, "Sherman was right. Wars just aren't a lot of yuks anymore."

The Eighth Day

It was shortly after midnight. In the command post briefing room Colonel Walker was addressing his staff.

"Gentlemen, that's the situation. Colonel Hambleton confirms that more mobile guns have been brought into the area since we plastered it yesterday. Charley's already back to work, and it's business as usual. That's why higher headquarters ruled out another Jolly Green rescue attempt. That area's too hot. We've got to get Hambleton out some other way.

"Make yourselves comfortable, gentlemen. Sandwiches and coffee will be brought in. We're not leaving this command post until we've come up with a plan to get him out of there without using choppers. So let's get on it." He turned to the intelligence officer. "Sam, kick it off."

Piccard crossed over to the wall map showing Hambleton's position, and tapped it with the stem of his pipe. "The Song Cam Lo River here is about two miles south of Hambleton's position. If we could get him to that river, he'd be away from the main roads the enemy is using. If he could float down it a dozen clicks, it turns east out of the firefight zone. There we'd have a much better chance of effecting a rescue. Choppers should be able to get in there with no sweat."

Walker studied the map. "Makes sense. Only one problem— between Hambleton and the river there are land mines, unfriendly villages, and entrenched guns. Not to mention a lot of Vietnamese soldiers. Just how do you propose to get him to the river? And without tipping off Charley?"

"That's the problem."

Walker turned to the assembled officers. "All right, gentlemen, that's our assignment. We have to come up with a plan to get Hambleton to the river. And we've got to do it fast. Let's get with it."

Hambleton sat in his hole listening to the drone of equipment moving down the highway cloaked by the protection of the forming fog.

His mind turned over the events of the past twenty-four hours. It had been a long day. For the most part it had been fairly quiet after the blistering attack brought in by Birddog.

He had been sure the attack was going to be followed by the Jolly Greens coming in to get him. But as the morning wore on with no word from Birddog and no sign of the rescue choppers, he knew they would not be coming. His optimism had slowly turned to depression. Even with the villagers gone so the planes could attack and all but level the villages, the echoes of the last bomb dropped by the F-4's had hardly died in the hills before the gomers again started hauling in mobile guns to replace those that had been knocked out. It was obvious there would be no cooling off. This would be a hot spot as long as he was in it; no way was this area ever going to become sanitized enough to bring in rescue choppers. No way.

He had probably signed his own death warrant; he had reported to Birddog on the new mobile guns being dug in immediately following the attack. If headquarters had been weighing the odds of risking the rescue helicopters on another mission, he had really tipped the scales of the decision-making process against himself. Sure enough, in midafternoon Birddog appeared to inform him that the Jolly Greens were not coming. But a new plan was being worked out.

A new plan. What the hell kind of a new plan? What could anyone do in a situation like this? Dreamers. And now to compound his problems, he had finished the last of his water. That was the bad part about being run back and forth through this wringer; it literally squeezed a man dry. He was also down to his last ear of corn. And the final ignominy, some bastardly F-4 pilot had put some eggs in too close and blown up his cornfield. That wasn't up to usual standards. He meant to talk to Birddog about that.

But there was one bright spot—if it could really be called bright. The attack had kept the gomers busy: Burying their dead, taking care of their wounded, reactivating their gun positions, and digging in again had kept them so occupied they hadn't gotten around to resuming their minesweeping operations. Still, they would, in spite of the fact they would have to start all over again. The Sandys had obliged, meanwhile, laying in several more loads of gravel, to fill in the weak spots in his protective barrier.

But now, almost one o'clock in the morning, Hambleton was feeling very sorry for himself. He was thirsty and hungry, so he decided to eat his last piece of corn. He shucked it, ate it very slowly, almost kernel by kernel, popping the juicy yellow buds with his teeth, relishing the liquid that slid down his throat.

So they were going to come up with a new plan. Why didn't they just give up? He was tying up half the Air Force, besides risking the lives of his fellow crewmen. Why didn't they just go home, leave him to pull the top over his hole, and forget the whole thing. More damned trouble than he was worth. And he was so tired ...

The buzzing of the Birddog snapped him out of his reverie. He switched on his radio. "Come in, Birddog. Bat Twenty-one."

"Roger, Bat. I've got a deal for you."

"Any deal I'll accept. I'm not in the world's greatest bargaining position."

"We're going to try something different."

"Anything is bound to be an improvement."

"You know exactly where you are, mapwise. Is that Roger?"

"Affirmative."

"Outstanding. The head shed has decided that you're going to have to make like Charley Tuna."

Hambleton's eyeballs rolled toward the heavens. This was gibberish.

"Acknowledge my transmission, Bat."

"Received your transmission. Trying to figure it out. You did say Charley Tuna."

"Roger."

"Give me a minute."

"You've got it."

Hambleton tried to clutch his sputtering brain into high gear. Charley Tuna? Charley Tuna? A code name for something? But what? What the hell? Then it came! The television commercial! He stroked his whiskers. Let's see. Charley Tuna and Star-Kist. That was it. Charley was the fish that wasn't good enough to make Star-

Kist, and he never got caught in spite of his best efforts. Fish. A fish that stayed in the water. What water? The river! That had to be it. They wanted him to get to the river. "I think I've got your message," he transmitted. "I think I follow you."

"Good. But just to be sure," the Birddog pilot launched into nasal but recognizable song. "Suwannneee, how I love ya, how I love ya, my dear ole Suwannneeee...."

Hambleton winced at the terrible rendition, but its meaning came through clear. Suwannee River. OK, he had to get to the river! And the Charley Tuna TV commercial. They wanted him to get *into* the river. The screwy code would throw off any gomers who were listening in. "Roger, Birddog. Understand."

"Outstanding."

"Stand by." As Birddog clicked compliance, Hambleton rummaged for his rubber map. He spread it out on his lap. As close as he could tell the river was a good two miles to the south of his position. He peeked over the top of his entrenchment. He could see a cluster of soldiers around a campfire in the remains of one of the villages. During the attack he had seen rifle fire coming from the copse of trees on his right, in the direction of the river. He knew the approximate location of at least three new guns that had been brought in and camouflaged. No telling what else would booby-trap him before he made it to the river. God, it wasn't going to be easy!

"This has to be your decision," said Birddog. "You can stay in place and we'll do our best to get you out of there eventually. But it'll be faster if you can get to where things are cooler."

"Understand."

"It's gonna be a sporty course. I don't need to tell you that."

"No, you don't."

"Think on it. Take your time making your decision."

"Wilco." Hambleton's head spun. He checked the notches he had made on his calendar stick. Seven. For a full week now he had been living in a hole. Five men had been lost trying for a rescue, aircraft had been tied up in an all-out effort to save him. The enemy would soon be returning to the land-mine sweepers. In another fog they could well get through to him. Time was on their side; the gomers called the shots. His food and water were gone. There was little likelihood of clearing out the guns for a chopper rescue, and he didn't want any more attempts made unless the odds were shifted considerably. He wasn't feeling all that great now, and his physical and mental strength would deteriorate the longer he stayed there. He made his decision.

"I'm with you, Birddog. We have to do something, even if it ain't too bright."

"Roger, Bat. We're working on a plan."

"I hope to hell it's a good one."

"When can you start?"

"Anytime. Just have to leave a note for the milkman."

"Outstanding. I'll get back to you with the plan. In the meantime get all the rest you can. You're gonna need it."

"Roger. One thing, Birddog. Gotta travel at night. No daylight or twilight."

"Understand, Bat. Be checking back soon. Birddog out."

Hambleton had now committed himself. The die was cast. He leaned back in his hole. Was this walking-out plan really possible? Didn't matter! It was goddamn grim, but it seemed the best deal.

What were the alternatives, anyway? Not much. Not a big helluva lot. The land-mine protection—period. That was all. No. He had made the right choice. Damned if he was going to stay in a hole and rot.

He carefully made his way to his vantage point. He looked out, studying the black terrain washed occasionally by the light of the waxing moon peeking through high stratus clouds. Some fog was creeping in on its belly, hugging the ground, but visibility was a little better than usual. It was fairly quiet. Except for the rumble of the traffic and the clank of tank treads on the highway, it could have been his Arizona moon. Next to the village to the east he could make out a small group of soldiers unloading something from a blacked-out truck. Probably more mine detectors to replace those that had been destroyed in the last attack.

Then he felt a surge of anxiety. Those land mines. How could they get him through the gravel? Hell, how? Except for a chopper or some great cherry picker that could reach across and pluck him from his hole, there was just no other way. The very defense that had kept the enemy at bay would surely keep him a prisoner in his small reservation.

He shook himself, shivering despite the sweat. Leave it to them! The powers back at the head shed must have something in mind. Birddog said they were working on a plan. All he could do was trust them. But even so, if he was to get through those mines, best he try and memorize the surrounding terrain.

Directly to the west were rice paddies several hundred feet square, surrounded by small ditches. Since the plowing had been done only recently, no rice had been planted and there was no water in the ditches. A narrow path ran along the top of the slight buildup between the ditches of each paddy. Here and there on the paths were small clumps of bushes, offering at least some protection in case he had to dive into one.

The freshly plowed ground offered another problem he had to remember. The imprint of his flying boots would be a dead giveaway; not too many Vietnamese soldiers wore size twelve boots. Anyone discovering his prints would know immediately the direction in which he was walking, and would be about as difficult to follow as a drunken bear. He was going to have to play it cool. Real cool.

And on the other side of the village, what lay there? What formidable trap would he stumble into? Aside from the gomers and the unfriendlies, what about snakes, poisonous insects, and other predators that sought refuge in the same dens as he? And what if ...

Oh hell, he had to cool it! Cross one bridge at a time. Make it through that mine field, then take on the other problems as they come. One at a time.

Back in his hole, he began preparations for his depature. He picked up his survival vest and took inventory. It would be wise to travel as light as possible. First, the pen-gun flares. They were small but they were also heavy; Birddog had told him they probably wouldn't be needed, so out they went. There were a few bills of Thai money. It was a good guess he wouldn't be doing a hell of a lot of shopping on the way to the river. Ditch 'em. Same with oxygen mask—not much use for an oxygen mask in the river, especially with no oxygen. The helmet? That took a little more mental debate. It had been good protection and had served as his pillow for a week. But it was too heavy and conspicuous. With some hesitancy he elected to leave it behind, too.

He would take his knife, revolver, first-aid kit, radio, and the other type of flares, gloves, and boots. And of course his eyeglasses. They had become a sort of fetish, a security blanket. Somehow he felt that as long as he had his specs, he would somehow muddle through. Besides, it wasn't cricket to hit anybody with glasses on.

Everything that was to stay behind he stuffed tightly into his helmet. He then put it in the bottom of the hole and covered it with the dirt he had dug out, even going so far as to transplant a small fern in the soft fill, so the spot would not be marked in a day or two by dying foliage. Then with an leafy branch he swept away his footprints, took one last long look at the spot in which he had spent the longest week in his life, and with no small sense of misgiving crawled to the edge of the clearing.

He pulled out his radio and waited for the message from Birddog.

Captain Clark entered the command post, squinting from the bright light and the blue haze of tobacco smoke that filled the room. He strode over to a table near the podium that bore up under a large coffee urn and a platter heaped with sandwiches. He poured himself a cup of coffee, picked up a ham on rye, and moved through the clusters of sweating staff officers to the wall map that was the focus of attention for Walker and another bird colonel. The other colonel was a stranger to Clark.

Walker acknowledged Clark's presence with a raise of his brows, and pointed to the latest reconnaissance photo of Hambleton's hiding place, which had been blown up to nearly wall-sized proportions. The other colonel was working on the map, drawing a zigzag course from Hambleton's dug-in position to the river. Clark watched silently for a moment. When he had fnished wolfing down his sandwich, Walker spoke up.

"Captain Clark, meet Colonel Ott."

"Glad to meet you, sir," said Clark.

"My pleasure, Captain," said Ott. "I understand you're Hambleton's FAC."

"One of 'em, sir."

"Guardian angels more like it." said Walker. "How is Hambleton?"

"Hard to tell, Colonel. He puts up a good front. Still has his sense of humor. When I asked him if he wanted to travel, he said all he had to do was leave a note for the milkman."

Ott grinned. "That sounds like the old bastard."

"Colonel Ott is an old golfing buddy of Hambleton's," said Walker. "He's come up with a plan to get Hambleton to the river."

"Outstanding," said Clark. "He's sitting on ready."

"I'm not too sure how outstanding the plan is," said Walker. "But we've had the wing staff locked up in this room since noon yesterday, when we got the word to stand down another Jolly Green attempt. The staff has come up with some real gems. We've considered everything from tunneling in to get him to dropping a balloon and helium pack so he could float out. I won't even tell you some of the others. It's been a long night."

"But you have come up with a plan?" said Clark.

Walker rubbed his eyelids with the tips of his fingers. "I guess you could call it a plan. It's pretty far out. But the staff agrees it's worth a try. I just hope to God it works. Frank, show Clark what we've come up with."

"Right," said Ott. "Clark, as Colonel Walker just told you, I'm an old golfing buddy of Hambleton's. We've played many a hole together. All over the world. I don't know if anyone ever told you, but Hambleton's one of the best golfers in the Air Force. Would you believe a five handicap? I hate the SOB. Anyway, come up here to the map and I'll explain the scheme."

Clark listened, studying the zigzag lines that had been drawn in on the plastic overlay. When Ott finished, Clark closed a mouth that had flopped open. Then he swallowed. "I think, gentlemen, that is the goddamndest plan I've ever seen!"

Hambleton lay in the brush, half dozing, fighting sleep lest he miss Birddog's call. For several hours he had lain there. In another couple hours it would be dawn. Should he start back to his hole, dig in before daylight came? Should he ... But there it was! The sound of Birddog's engines. Praise Allah!

He tried to quell the tremor in his voice. "Bat Twenty-one here, Birddog."

"Roger, Bat, QSY to Delta channel."

He switched his radio to *D* channel. "On Delta."

"Roger, Bat. In case the gooks find this discrete frequency, keep your transmissions short."

"Wilco."

"Ready to spread your wings?"

"Spirit's willing."

"Outstanding. Now you know your destination?"

"Affirmative."

"Rog. And we're going to get you there. Understand you're quite a golfer."

Hambleton blinked, then stared at his radio. "Say again, Birddog."

"Golf, Bat. Understand you play golf."

"Sure I play golf."

"And you've played a lot of the big courses."

What the hell was Birddog doing? "Know a lot of courses. Yes."

"I hope you remember them."

"I do." He had always made it a point to remember the courses and the holes. Like a good salesman, a golfer has to know the territory.

"Outstanding. Because we're about to play a brisk eighteen holes."

That did it. Hambleton stared at his radio in disbelief. Was he dreaming all this? The FAC pilot was crazy. Too much strain, weird things happen to pilots who jazz their throttles too much. "Play a golf game?"

"Affirmative. With your old golf crony, Colonel Frank Ott."

Frank Ott! That old scoundrel! What the hell? He wasn't even in the theater!

"Do you read, Bat?"

"I read." I'm going to play eighteen holes with Frank Ott. I'll get my clubs."

"Sooner you tee off the better. Maybe we can get several holes in before daylight. Let me know when you're ready."

Hambleton's eyeballs beseeched the heavens for assistance. Good God! It was obvious the young pilot had really flipped.

"Our first hole is number one at Tucson National."

Wait a minute. Birddog's voice didn't sound crazy. "You say I'm to tee off on hole number one of the Tucson National Golf Course."

"Roger. Before you start be damned sure you line your shot up properly. Very bad traps on this hole."

"Stand by, Birddog. Discussing this shot with my caddy."

"Take your time, Bat."

"Roger." Now let's see, he had to go at this thing analytically. He was supposed to get to the river. If he could float down it a ways, he'd get out of this firefight furnace. And to get to the Suwannee he was going to play eighteen holes of golf. And the first hole was to be the number-one hole at Tucson National. Now why number one at Tucson?

He thought back to the beautiful course out northwest of the city. There it lay, a robe of green on the lap of those purple-pink mountains. He had played the course a hundred times with old Frank Ott. But why the course at Tucson? And why number-one hole?

Wait! That hole was long and straight. And it was several hundred yards in length—430 yards, to be exact. And with sand traps. Why not the seventh hole? It was about the same length. Why not ... and then it hit him. Direction! That was it, *direction!* Number one at Tucson goes southeast! And southeast was roughly in the direction of the river. Goddamn! That's it! Birddog wasn't crazy. He was brilliant!

What a plan! Probably inspired by Frank Ott or another of his old golfing cronies. This was the code they would use so as not to tip off the enemy. A gomer would no more know the direction of the first hole at Tucson National than Hambleton would know the route of a Vietcong sampan race.

His yo-yo spirits climbed up the string. Thank God he was a navigator. It was second nature for him to know directions. He even wore a small compass on a string around his neck when he played golf. And there were a good half-dozen courses he could sit down right now and draw from memory, give or take a few degrees on the lay of the holes. "Birddog from Bat Twenty-one. Ready to tee off."

There was a marked lilt in Birddog's response. "From the sound of your voice, I think you know what we're trying to do."

"I think I do."

"Outstanding. One word of caution. Be sure of hole number one. It will take you through the gravel. The last F-4 strike chopped a narrow corridor through the tulip field."

"Roger."

There was a pause, then, "Good luck, Bat Twenty-one."

"Thanks, Birddog. Teeing off now."

"Fore!" came back the crisp reply.

Hambleton stood erect behind one of the trees that bordered his refuge. A gamut of emotions rippled through him: fear at leaving his sanctuary; elation at starting off on a positive project that just might lead to freedom; a touch of euphoria as he stood erect, acting like a human being instead of the stalked animal he had been for the past seven days.

He looked around. The moon had been blocked out by high clouds, and the terrain in front of him was india ink, dabbled with gray spots of fog. Only an orange glow in the southwest intruded on the darkness, marking the long wooden bridges that planes had set afire the night before. It was an eerie, foreboding yet enticing netherworld.

He pulled out his compass. He knew the bearing of the first hole and he understood Birddog's confirming hint about the tulip field. In the darkness he barely made out the heading of 135 degrees southeast. Sighting along it, he fixed on the shadowy outline of a distant clump of brush. He took his golfer's stance—a small, incongruous smile playing his lips—and flexed his body. There was stiffness in every muscle, but he concentrated on his form ... feet just so ... keep that arm straight ... then he swung back an imaginary club and whacked the invisible ball.

Right down the middle. "Now following through," he muttered. "Hot damn, Hambone, Let's go!"

He started out. He headed into no-man's-land. Softly, carefully, he planted each step. Feeling his way more than seeing it, his breath locked in his chest for fear of making noise, each footfall was an eternity. Praying that his rescuers had the right fix on the gravel corridor, he crept painfully forward, using protesting muscles and bones that had done little but soak up dampness for a week. He had paced off enough putts to know his normal stride was roughly a yard, and he counted steps as he went, stopping often to check his compass.

His vision adapted to the darkness, yet he could barely make out the scrubby brush. "Just keep watching that brush, moving straight toward it," he kept telling himself over and over, endeavoring to take his mind off the land mines. It wasn't easy. Visions of the soldiers mangled by the insidious explosives kept swimming through his head. True, the F-4's were good, but there was no guarantee that they had destroyed all the mines in the corridor. This damn fairway still might have some hidden traps in it.

Stopping often, listening, sniffing the wind, he spotted movement to the south. The soldiers had recovered from the fierce attack earlier. They were now preparing to resume their minesweeping. They were hundreds of yards away, but even so he quickened his strides.

After thirty minutes of this he was tiring fast. The unaccustomed exertion, the terrible strain of being on the constant alert for gravel and gomers was taking its toll. He had to rest soon. He counted off the approximate number of yards the first hole should be just as he came to a fork of a path that ran off in two directions. The clump of brush was exactly at the intersection. He plopped into it, sat listening quietly for any signs of detection. Then he clicked on his radio and whispered into it.

"Birddog from Bat Twenty-one. Estimate end of first hole."

"Roger, Bat Twenty-one. You near a fork in the fairway?"

"Affirmative."

"Congratulations. Hole in one. Didn't see any explosions, so you musta stayed out of the sand traps. Now some of these holes you'll be playing may not make sense to you. But there's a reason for them. For one, we're trying to keep you out of soft fairways. Golf-shoe divots would be a red flag. So watch 'em."

Hambleton clicked an acknowledgment.

"Ready for the next hole?"

He clicked his transmitter again.

"Roger. Next is hole number five at Davis Monthan."

Hambleton thought for a moment. The fifth hole at Davis Monthan Air Base went due east. About four hundred yards. Not a difficult hole. He checked his compass, took a deep breath, and started out on a heading of ninety degrees. He could just make out the outlines of a grove of trees in the distance and he began counting his strides.

His eyes were adjusting better to the night. He could see a narrow path underfoot, small bushes to either side. He was sure he was out of the gravel area by now, and this made him breathe a little easier. Roughly forty minutes later, the number of strides clicked off, he looked around him. There was the small copse of trees several paces away. He made a dive for it.

He hadn't realized what poor shape he was in. He sat for a moment, waiting for his lungs to catch up. Then he called the FAC with his progress report.

"Outstanding," said Birddog. "Another hole in one?"

"Would you believe four strokes?"

"Jack Nicklaus you ain't. But here's a chance to improve your score. Next hole is number five at Shaw Air Force Base."

"Roger. Number five at Shaw." While he caught his breath, Hambleton concentrated. Number five at the air base curved slightly to the northeast. He checked his compass, lining up the hole. He checked it again, looking puzzled. That course would take him toward the village to the east—a village that had been heavily fortified. True, the last fighter attack had beat it up, but this was the one with the guns that had knocked down the chopper. It had better be deserted now. Birddog and the intelligence types must know more about it than he did. Or had he made a miscalculation playing one of his holes?

No. Birddog was monitoring his progress, and so far he had been right on target. He would have been warned if he had strayed. He had to play their game; Birddog was following his exact position by triangulating the clicks of his radio. He just hoped to hell the gomers weren't doing the same thing.

He started out on his third hole. It *was* taking him toward that village! After pacing off two hundred yards, he had to stop and rest. He wasn't getting very good mileage to an ear of corn. He squatted in the middle of the path, studying the village. Sure enough, the green at the end of this hole was right at the village edge. But the next hole would probably veer around it.

Doggedly he got back on his feet and walked on, crouching low, clicking off his yards. At what he considered the green of his third hole there was a good-sized clump of bushes in a paddy slightly off to his left. He got down on his hands and knees and crawled to it, so as not to make any tracks in the soft ground. Inside he sat quietly for a moment, listening. Strange. Not a sound. This was eerie. Was everyone asleep, or had the bulk of the soldiers moved south with the war? So far this had been easy. Maybe too easy.

He checked in with Birddog.

"Roger, Bat. How are you holding up?"

"Dark down here. Keep losing my balls."

"Don't lose your balls now. Gonna need 'em. Ready for your fourth hole?"

"Just about."

"Roger. Remember the fourteenth at the Masters?"

How could anyone forget that hole? It was one always shown on television during the Masters tournament. Many a time Hambleton had sat, beer in hand, nose glued to the tube, watching the tournament play. The fourteenth hole, especially, was a tough one. "Remember it well, Birddog. It's mean. Lots of traps."

"Roger. Remember that. Lots of traps."

Hambleton conjured the course in his mind's eye. Hole number fourteen at the Augusta National Golf Club goes—let's see—east by northeast. With a slight dogleg to the left. He'd have to watch that, make sure of his compass headings. Par-four hole, over four hundred yards. Four twenty, to be exact. He sighted in with his compass. What the hell? *It went smack through the village!*

Had Birddog goofed this time? Damn, it would be nice if he could discuss the village with Birddog. But that was out. It could be a direct tip-off to any gomer who might be monitoring.

"Birddog, confirm. Fourteenth hole at the Masters?"

There was a pause, while Birddog obviously rechecked his chart. "That is affirmative. Again, beware of the traps."

So it was right. The planners had evidently meant for him to go right through the village. But why? It would be just as easy to circumvent it. Go around it on either side. Longer, yes, but it should be considerably safer. Unless there was something on both sides of the village.

Well, they should know. They had their intelligence. And he had seen the photo planes flying many passes over his hole, often at altitudes so high they were scarcely visible to the naked eye. But with the advanced state of the art of photo reconnaissance, altitude was no problem. He himself had seen a flight-line photo of his base taken from more than six miles up. With its high resolution and fine grain, the photo had been magnified to the point where it was possible to tell the winning hand in a group of maintenance men playing poker near one of the hangars. Yes, the photo-analysis experts must have studied the reccy photos, and together with their other intelligence data, they would know more about the terrain than he did.

Still, you never underestimated the gomers. These were mainly North Vietnamese Regulars, a tough, hard-hitting, shrewd, well-trained bunch. They were masters in the art of camouflage. He had seen enemy soldiers dressed so deceivingly in their foliage that they looked more like a bush than a bush did. And some camouflage could not be detected, even with infrared cameras. Like the gun that had shot down the chopper. And the ...

Oh hell, on with Birddog's ball game. There was only room for one quarterback on a team. Trust them. He was tired, enervated, and dehydrated. At this point he could screw anything up. He just had to listen to Birddog upstairs. Besides, he had old Frank Ott playing in this twosome, and Ott wouldn't let him down.

But just in case, he whispered into his radio: "One thing, Birddog. If the course becomes crowded it may not be possible to use the radio. If I get caught in a sand trap I'll use the beeper, but no words. If I can't blast out of the trap I'll give you a long beep before destroying my radio."

"Roger, Bat Twenty-one." Birddog's voice was subdued.

Destroying the radio! Asinine! God knows, the gomers had plenty they had captured from downed flyers. But damned if he was going to make another contribution—add to their list of frequencies used by the Air Force. He'd play the rule of conduct: Resist capture and destroy your radio.

For a quarter of an hour Hambleton sat and watched the village, alert for any sound. There was none. No movement at all. Not even the oink of a pig or the crowing of a rooster. No fires, no smell of food cooking. Tombstone. Silent City.

The first tint of dawn was beginning to brush the horizon. OK, it was time to get a move on. He couldn't waste any more valuable time. This would be a most critical hole. Maybe win or lose the game. Remember, keep your head down and watch your swing. Follow through. Now let's get on with the game.

"Birddog from Bat Twenty-one. Teeing off on the fourth now."

"Roger, Bat Twenty-one."

The Ninth Day

In the Pentagon the Chairman of the Joint Chiefs of Staff put down his ball-point. "Hold it. Just a minute, Colonel. Would you please run that by again."

The intelligence officer stopped in the middle of his prepared briefing. "Yes, sir. From what point, sir?"

"A few sentences back. Did I understand you to say that Hambleton is getting to the river *by playing golf?*"

"Yes, Admiral. I had it verified. It's true."

"Would you mind expanding on that?"

"Actually, the idea came out of a skull session at the 388th Wing. It was approved by Seventh Air Force. An imaginary eighteen-hole golf course was overlaid on the latest reconnaissance photo strip of Hambleton's area. It was designed to provide the safest route around enemy camps, gun emplacements and unfriendly villages. The first nine holes get him to the Song Cam Lo River. The back nine he'll make floating down the river."

"I don't believe it," said the Chairman.

"It's true, sir. As of dawn, Vietnam time, Hambleton completed the first four holes without incident. He's now resting up until darkness so he can continue the game."

"I assume the FAC pilot is feeding him the information."

"Yes, sir. Hole by hole. It's very doubtful the North Vietnamese can understand golf language, even if they do pick up the radio frequency being used."

Admiral Moorer turned to the Air Force Chief of Staff. "John, that's the damnedest thing I've ever heard! Who wrote the ops plan, Alfred Hitchcock?"

General Ryan grinned. "When the idea began to jell, some of Hambleton's old golfing partners were contacted. They all contributed. Besides his golf buddies at Tucson and Vietnam, they also contacted a friend of his in Hawaii and Colonel Don Buchholz here at the Pentagon. It seems Hambleton is quite a golfer."

Moorer shook his head. "He'd better be! Damned clever. Let's get a copy of that course. I want to follow his progress personally."

"Copy's on the way, sir" said the intelligence officer.

"Good. And let's clamp a tight security on this one. If it works, we might be able to use it again."

"Yes, sir."

Moorer sighed. "Why not a crazy golf game in the middle of a lunatic war? Makes sense to me."

Hambleton checked his watch. A little past midnight. It would soon be time. He stretched quietly, arching the stiffness from his back. It had been a restless day with not much sleep.

Things could be so quiet at night and so lively during the day. Last night on his trip through the village—his fourth hole—the gutted buildings could have been a deserted movie set of plaster and chicken wire. He had not seen a soul. Only one small incident had marred his progress: He had stumbled over something in the dark that had turned out to be a dead pig. Even this buoyed his spirits. If there had been anyone around, the pig would surely have been roasting over some village fire instead of rotting in the street.

He had clicked off the yardage of the Masters' fourteenth hole, and found himself near a shed at the outskirts of the village. It was here he now lay, under a pile of hay, waiting for the blanket of darkness to hide his next movements.

Although the night had been tomb quiet, the day had been something else. He could still hear the rumble of war equipment heading south on the nearby highway. About noon he had awakened with a start to the smell of Vietcong cooking and the pleasant aroma of tea wafting his way from a nearby hooch that was by then occupied by a dozen soldiers. Perhaps a crew that manned one of the mobile antiaircraft guns just being brought in. Thank God, he had thought, the Air Force had voted against bringing in any more Jolly Greens. They would have been reduced to scrap metal by all the artillery the Vietcong had dug in hereabouts.

As dusk had turned into evening and evening into night, the village had again quieted. The evening meals over, the soldiers could be heard laughing and talking for a while. But with few lamps, no electric lights, and little to do, they soon turned in, and one by one the camp fires flickered out. Rales of snoring then replaced the chatter.

No attacking planes came in to interrupt the reverie. Except for some far-off noise of troops—judged by Hambleton to be the crews manning the mine detectors—all was quiet on the northern front. Almost peaceful.

Evidently the gomers hadn't yet discovered fairway one or worked their way through the mine field and found him missing. If they had, the place would now be crawling with search parties. But they would eventually get through, and the more distance he could put between himself and his former homestead, the safer he would be. It was time to shake a leg.

He crawled out from under the hay and sat a moment, listening. His mouth tasted like a newspaper from the bottom of a parakeet cage. God, he was thirsty! How long had it been since his water ran out? He picked up a piece of straw and started chewing it to get saliva going. He was so hungry he could have eaten a horse. He patted his flat stomach. At least Gwen would be proud of him; he could forget Weight Watchers for a hell of a long time. He checked his watch again. Twelve-twenty. Time for his prearranged check-in with Birddog. He flicked on his radio.

Birddog answered immediately. "How goes it, Bat Twenty-one?"

"Tolerable. Thirsty and hungry. Stomach thinks my throat's cut."

"Understand, Bat. We've got plans for that. Ready to tee off?"

"Ball's all teed up."

"Outstanding. This time we'll play an interesting hole. Abilene Country Club. Hole number four. Ring a bell?"

Something surfaced through the fog in Hambleton's mind and exploded like a skyrocket. "Ring a bell? You kidding?"

"Thought it might."

"I shot a hole in one on that hole."

"I know."

"There was a nice breeze coming in from the west. Early morning. I used a number-five wood and—"

"Never mind." Birddog chuckled. "I don't want to hear about it. I just want you to repeat it."

"Roger." How in hell did Birddog know about his hole in one? Frank Ott? He hadn't been there. Who *had* been with him that day? He racked his brain. Gwen? Who else had been there? Wilson? Allison? Good Lord, they must have chased down every old golf buddy he had! Bless 'em!

"Waiting, Bat. Or do you want me to play on through?"

"Roger, Birddog. Teeing off now."

Enough ruminating. He had to concentrate on his game. Number four at Abilene went due east, straight as an arrow, 195 yards. He took out his compass and sighted. The course would take him through the outskirts of the village and into the darkness toward the river. He felt a pang of fear. The first four holes had been through known territory. He had spent a week in the security of his hole studying the terrain. But now a whole new ball game. He was moving out into the unknown, and had no idea of the situation beyond the village.

Well, it was time to find out. Cautiously he left the shed, scouting for every twig, branch, anything that might snap underfoot and alert the nearby troops. On leopard's feet he crouched along in the darkness, checking his compass heading, counting his strides. He was coming to the end of the main road that ran through the village, and the earth was turning softer. He sought harder ground.

Must be careful of prints; stay on the beaten path, the hard ground. Probaby the reason he had been routed through the village instead of around it. Or maybe it was two reasons: The main street would register no prints with its mess of foot and vehicle tracks, and the village would be the last place anyone would look for him if his empty hole had been found. Damned clever, those Yankees back at the head shed.

He had clicked off a hundred yards. Time to rest a spell, listen, and reconnoiter. There was a small hooch just up ahead. He would make that and blend in with its fleeting shadows, cast by the near-half moon. The hut had been gutted, its roof caved in; it was obviously deserted. He sneaked up to the doorway and was just on the verge of ducking in when a violent movement erupted in the shadows.

A chicken came flopping out of the doorway, clucking and scolding. Hambleton dropped to his knees, his pulse banging. The scrawny bird emitted several more cackles and landed in the street. Hambleton watched it, trying to get back to seminormalcy. Good Christ! Enough to give a person apoplexy.

And then his fear was suddenly overtaken by something stronger—hunger. God! Chicken! Meat! Food! Man, would it taste good! Even if he had to eat it raw!

Crouching in the shadows by the doorway, he watched and waited. The bird was strutting along, pecking at the gravel in the ditch on his side of the road, its long neck jerking spasmodically, coming closer. As it neared, in the dim light Hambleton saw his chicken turn into a rooster—a tall, strutting, skinny bird, its comb hanging oddly down over one eye. It would be tough as shoe leather. Never mind. He was a hell of a lot tougher. He brought out his knife, and poised to spring.

Come on! That's it! Just a little closer! He had to make his first strike count. He would dispatch it quickly, unerringly. He had to keep the noise to an absolute minimum.

He sprang! But as he did, another shadow also hurtled out of the darkness. Hambleton, launching his flying tackle on the bird, felt rather than saw the human figure erupt from the hooch. It was on a collision course. The rooster took off squawking bloody murder as Hambleton wrestled with the body that had slammed into him. Then his eye caught the glint of a knife in the moonlight, and he felt a sharp pain in his left shoulder.

Hambleton broke away and sprang to his feet, his adrenaline pumping power into tired limbs. He crouched, knife in hand. The figure sprang at him again, blade raised high. Hambleton thrust out his own and plunged forward, aiming directly at the upper midsection of the charging body. He connected. Even in the darkness he could see the look of surprise on the slant-eyed face as the leaping form suddenly froze in midflight. There was a muffled "ooooff!" and then the raised hand, still clutching the knife, slowly fell.

For a moment they were face to face, Hambleton swimming in the reek of fish oil coming from a mouth inches from his nostrils. Then, almost in slow motion, the body slid down Hambleton's rigid torso and came to rest in a crumpled heap at his feet.

Frozen in shock, Hambleton stared in mute horror at the figure on the ground. A wave of nausea engulfed him. And then, panic! His brain reeling, he looked around wildly. He spun and raced headlong down the road, succumbing to the irrational hope that distance would ameliorate the terror.

On he raced, panic propelling a body that had already suffered too much abuse, muscles protesting their strain, lungs rebelling with terrible chest pains. On he plowed, stumbling, falling, rolling over in the dust, only to remount shaking limbs to take him away—far away—from the unspeakable horror.

"Stop it! Stop it! You can't blow it now. You can't blow it now. Calm down. Calm down."

He staggered on, slowing, his body wracking. Completely spent, he stopped, sagging to his knees. He rolled over on his back, spread-eagled, and lay still as the panic ebbed. All he could hear then was the rasping noise of his lungs, the pounding of his heart in his ears. For some reason images of Gwen were dancing in his overwrought brain.

He looked up at the sky, his eyes trying to bring the moon into focus.

Gwen Hambleton bent down and recovered her golf ball from the cup. "Marge, would you believe a six on that hole?"

Marge smiled. "Let's see. A six divided by two is a three. We *are* making progress."

"Just put down the six."

"Six it is." Marge put the scorecard in her pocket and picked up her clubs. Together they strode toward the tee-off position for the next hole. "You're not sorry you came, are you, Gwen?"

"No, Marge. I'm glad I came. It's good to get out of the house."

"Beats clawing the wallpaper."

"Marge, do you believe in ESP?"

Marge turned to look at her friend. "I guess I'm not a believer. Not much of an occult nut, as far as that goes. But like everyone else, I have had strange things happen. Why do you ask?"

"Oh, nothing. I shouldn't even bring it up."

"Nonsense. Bring it up. Let's kick it around."

"Well, I know this sounds crazy. But on that last hole we just played—oh, never mind. It's silly."

"Nothing's silly between friends." She patted Gwen's hand. "Tell Mama Wilson all about it."

"You'll laugh."

"So I'll laugh."

"All right. It was back there. When my ball sliced into the sand trap. While I was setting up for the next shot, I could have sworn I heard Gene calling me. From the woods near the hole. It was almost like he was in some kind of trouble."

"Really?"

Gwen nodded. "It was so real! I actually found myself calling to him. It was like he needed help."

Marge mulled this. "Has it happened before?"

"Yes, it's happened before."

"And did it turn out to be anything serious?"

"Not really, no."

"There you are. I'll have to confess it's happened to me too. I've bolted up in the night, out of a deep sleep, just knowing Dick was in some kind of trouble." She smiled at her friend. "Maybe it's just part of being married to a man in a hazardous profession. This crazy flying business. Perhaps living with constant danger, as we do, brings a man and wife closer together."

Gwen fumbled in her golf bag for a Kleenex. "It's this crazy war. This insanity." She looked into Marge's eyes. "I haven't told anyone about this. But yesterday I got some hate mail. A terrible letter, saying they were glad my husband was shot down. That it served him right for being over there. As if Gene were responsible for the whole thing."

"Oh, my God!"

"I just don't understand. Gene's one of the most gentle people on this earth. He'll shoo a fly out the door before he'll swat it. And to be called those horrible names—"

"Who sent the letter?"

"It was unsigned, of course. Postmarked San Francisco."

"Gwen, dear, don't you even think about it. Tear that letter up. Don't give it a second thought."

"I've already destroyed the letter. I just wish I could erase it from my mind."

Marge shook her head. "It's so unreal. I've been reading in the papers about widows and wives of POWs getting this kind of mail.

What kind of depraved mind would dream up that kind of hate campaign?"

"I'm sorry I mentioned it. I didn't mean to bring it up." She dabbed at her eyes. "It's just that we were talking about Gene and this funny feeling I had about him." She stood, stuffing the Kleenex into her pocket. "We won't let it spoil your morning."

"We won't let it spoil *our* morning."

As they picked up their clubs, Marge turned to Gwen. "About that ESP. When you said you felt as if Gene were right there with you. Do you know what I'm thinking?"

"What?"

"ESP can work both ways, so I'm told."

Gwen brightened. "That is a comforting thought. Gene and I have always been very close. Yes. That is a happy thought."

"Good," said Marge smiling. "Now, let's play golf."

In the flight-line maintenance shack, Captain Clark poured himself a cup of coffee and plunked down on the decrepit divan. He was just lighting a cigarette when Colonel Walker strode in. Clark started to rise. "Morning, Colonel."

"Keep your seat. Mind if I grab a cup of coffee and join you?"

"Be my guest."

Walker crossed over to the coffee bar, returned with a cup and sat down beside Clark. He looked at his watch. "Four A.M. That's what I love about the Air Force. The good hours."

Clark poked back a spring that had popped up through a cushion of the ancient divan. "Not to mention the luxury."

"Enjoying your leave?"

"Having a ball."

"Great spot for a vacation." He cast a glance at the FAC pilot. "You getting your crew rest, Clark?"

"Yes, sir. I've been sacking out during the day. When Colonel Hambleton holes up."

Walker grunted. "Just got a sketchy report from Apache Control about Hambleton. How about filling me in?"

Clark took a deep drag from his cigarette. "He's going to turn my hair white. Really scared hell out of me on the fifth hole."

"The fifth. The one past the village."

"Right. For a full hour after he was supposed to complete the hole I couldn't raise him. It was really getting ulcer time. That's when I notified Apache Control."

"Go on."

"Then I finally got an acknowledment from him. He seemed to be real spooked—quiet and subdued for the first time. Like somebody had just kicked him in the solar plexus. Wasn't like the old duffer at all."

"So he had a problem on that hole. Could you make out what happened?"

"It was pretty sketchy because of radio security. He said he'd had a run-in with another player. The other player lost."

"You think he might have bumped into the enemy? Had a fight?"

"That's my guess."

"Any injuries?"

"Said he picked up a flesh wound. Nothing serious."

"That poor bastard!"

Clark sighed. "He's had more than his share. That's for sure."

"Where is he now?"

"Just finished the seventh. The green on that one is the pigpen behind a deserted farmhouse. He's hiding under a slop trough."

"A slop trough?"

"I presume that's what he meant. Where the oink-oink imbibe, as he put it. Said he preferred it to the compost pile."

"Jesus Christ! Some choice."

"Ain't it."

Walker sipped on his coffee. "How's his physical condition?"

"Frankly, Colonel, I'm worried. He's sounding beat. He still tries to cover it up with a little bravado, but the voice is weak."

"How about his morale?"

"I'm sure it's worse than he lets on. He's very thirsty. It's been a couple of days without water, and all that exertion—it's telling."

"It's so damn frustrating!" Walker's fist came down on the makeshift coffee table. "So goddamned *frustrating!* There's that gutsy old fart out there in a pigsty dying of thirst, and we can't do a damn thing about it!"

"Do you think we might risk a drop? Get a CARE package to him?"

"We can't even do that! Just got word from the snoopers that the Charleys are through the mine field. I think we missed one.

Should have had Sandys keep dropping gravel. Now soon as they discover their bird's flown the coop they'll pull out all the stops to find him. If we dropped a CARE package now we would pinpoint his exact position. We can't take that chance."

"No, if that's the case, we sure can't risk a drop now."

"If he can only make it through the eighth hole he's got a fighting chance. Does he know about the eighth hole?"

"I've only dared hint at it. Don't want to clue in the enemy."

"Right. You can't be too careful over the radio." Walker took a large swig, then looked over at Clark. "By the way, are you a religious man, Denny?"

"Sort of. In my own weird fashion."

"Well, I am, Denny. In this business it helps. You need everything you can get going for you. My padre is Protestant. But I've also got that old rabble-rouser, Father O'Flynn, working on this one. And I'd get a rabbi working on it too, if I could find one."

"Excuse me, Captain," another voice broke in. The men looked up at the sergeant in the doorway. "Your plane is serviced. Ready to go."

"Thanks, Hank," said Clark, butting his cigarette and taking a last slug of coffee. "Well, Colonel, back to the links. If I never take up golf, you'll know the reason why. See you later." He headed for the door.

"Just one thought, Denny."

"Yes, sir?"

"No matter who you worship or how, what about pitchin' one in there for old Hambleton?"

"You're too late, Colonel."

"Too late?"

"Roger. I started that a week ago."

Hambleton checked his watch. About time to punch in with Birddog. He crawled out from under the pig trough and sat up, trying to peer through the darkness.

For the first time he really became aware of the overpowering stench of the pigsty. When he had collapsed in it hours earlier, he had been so numb his senses hadn't even registered the odor. Maybe now, on the balance, he was slightly more alive than dead.

He unzipped his flying suit down to his waist, and pulled

down the sleeve on the side of his injured shoulder. The wound had stopped bleeding. It was not a deep cut, probably due to the thick nylon webbing of his survival vest, which had helped deflect the assailant's knife. For a while it had hurt like blazes, but now it seemed to itch more than throb. He produced his first-aid kit and dressed the wound as best he could.

Try as he might, he could not drive the horror of the fifth hole from his mind. Actually killing a man face to face had been the most terrifying thing he had ever done in his life. Who was that guy? Who was it who had leaped on him from out of the darkness? A North Vietnamese soldier, more than likely. But if so, where were his comrades? Could he have been a lone soldier on patrol? Or, God forbid, could he have been a fugitive like himself? Maybe a sympathetic villager who had not elected to flee with the evacuees, and who had stayed behind to harass the Communists, trying to live off the land? It was this thought that got to him. It had been too dark to make out the man's clothing.

The whole thing could have been a grim coincidence—just two hungry, tired guys stalking the same chicken, then colliding in the night. And he had killed the man, snuffed out a human life. Sure, it had been self-defense. Had he not been the quicker, the other would certainly have dispatched him, no question about that. Yet somehow, none of this made it any easier.

On top of that, he had broken the key rule of survival training. He had panicked. For the first time, he had panicked. He had thrown rationality to the winds, had galloped off like a wild fool, expending precious energy, becoming completely disoriented. So much so that when he regained his composure, he had had to retrace his steps to reorient himself. This was not only inexcusable, but very risky.

It worried him. He had always been considered a cool cat. As a navigator—a vital member of a flying crew—the whole success of a mission often depended upon him. He was just naturally expected to keep his head under pressure, to think soundly and analytically no matter what the stresses. And in his whole career he had never let the team down.

But now he had committed a flat-out, bald-assed act of complete irrationality. There were extenuating circumstances, but nothing—absolutely nothing—justified what he had done. Especially when his very life depended on it. He had to get a grip on himself. A good grip. So starting right now, he was going to shape up!

He forced himself to concentrate. First, there was the body. It would certainly be found at daylight, if not before. And if the gomers had broken through the mine field and had discovered he was gone, they would damn well put two and two together and start combing the area. He was utterly pooped from the last two holes, but he had to get the hell out of there. The more distance he could put between him and that body, the better.

He repacked his first-aid kit, put it back in his survival vest, and clicked on his radio. Birddog responded immediately.

"How you doin', Bat Twenty-one?"

"I've felt better. The nap helped. Very dehydrated."

"Understand. We're going to do something about that. On this hole there's a refreshment stand. It's a short hole, par three. Number four at Corona de Tucson. No problem for an old pro."

He knew that course, south of Tucson, well. "Refreshment stand?"

"You'll understand when you get there. Just remember, you have to tap your own keg."

Oh, crap! Hambleton wiped his brow with a weary hand. A refreshment stand on his eighth hole. Have to tap your own keg. He was getting too tired to play this game of twenty questions much longer.

"Roger, Birddog. Teeing off."

"Sorry about the condition of the green on that last hole. But you'll like the next one."

"Roger. Bat out."

Hambleton took a bead on his compass and started, counting his strides, finding it took a massive effort just to put one foot ahead of the other. But he had two things going for him, two reference ponts to help in his orientation: the lights of Dang Ha to the north and those of Quang Tri to the southeast. Their reflections in the overhanging clouds were somehow heartening, and he did not have to squint at his compass in the dark so often.

He scuffed along for an eon, feeling the hard ground, weaving like a drunk trying to pass a sobriety test. As he walked the hole he noticed for the first time he seemed to be suffering from some disfunction he could not identify. His body kept tipping and falling backward; to compensate, he walked with his head forward. It made him feel like an Arizona roadrunner, but at least he kept his equilibrium.

For the last couple of days in his foxhole he had noticed he was having trouble raising his head above ground level when he was in a prone position. It had not alarmed him; he had merely chalked it up to his inactivity. But now, struggling through the darkness, the problem was giving him some concern. Could he have a neck injury? A back injury? Had something snapped when he blasted out of the airplane in his ejection seat? Well, to hell with it. Whatever it was, the ailment would just have to wait, stay on the back burner for the time being. He was too thirsty to care. He couldn't even spit cotton.

Another fifty yards and he would be on the green. The going was getting rough underfoot. He stopped to get his breath, check his compass, and study the terrain. He was coming to a wooded area dead ahead. The green of the eighth hole must be in the middle of that grove. He started out again, struggling more and more to keep his equilibrium. He was tripping, falling, getting up. He was disgusted with himself for not being able to control his body as he traversed the rough ground.

Finally he was in the woods, a banana grove dense with thick banana leaves. He thrust through it, clicked off the hundredth yard, then leaned against the trunk of a large banana plant and slid to the ground. He looked around, his tired eyes trying to penetrate the thick grove. So this was the hole with the refreshment stand, right? Well, he had news for Birddog. The catering truck hadn't shown up. There was no water here. There was nothing. Not even bananas. Either it wasn't the growing season, or the crop had been harvested.

He leaned his head against the tree and closed his eyes. He wondered idly if Birddog had tricked him, had lied to him just to keep him going, to click off one more yard, to push him to try and make one more objective. Well, screw him. Hambleton was pretty sure he'd never make it to the next hole, no matter what Birddog did.

He was imagining things again. Dehydrated as he was, his ears were gurgling. He shook his head to clear it, but the noise persisted. Hold it. If it was a flight of fancy, it sure as hell seemed real. He placed his ear hard against the banana tree. There it was again.

Hambone, you stupid ox! You have to tap your own keg! Of course! He was leaning against a keg of the sweetest water in the world. Anybody who had ever attended snake school knew that.

He whipped out his knife, the lesson of survival school filtering through his benumbed brain. In a banana tree the water flows up the trunk early in the morning and runs down to the ground at night. He had actually heard the water running. He stabbed his knife up to its hilt into the soft trunk three times, and pulled out a long triangular plug. Out spurted a small stream of water. He flopped down on his back, his mouth under the hole, and gulped like a beached flounder.

Sweet mother of Jesus, did that taste good! Clean, cool nectar of the heavens, cascading down his parched throat, splashing on his dirty face. Never had anything tasted so good. He drank long and hard, almost feeling the life-giving liquid being absorbed by parched tissues and dusty glands, flowing through his dehydrated body. It even seemed to rejuvenate his thinking processes. He plugged the hole, reached into his first-aid kit for his salt pills, took two, and drank some more.

When the water gave out he went to another plant, tapped it like a keg, and wet his handkerchief from the dribbling spring. He zipped down his flying suit and gave himself a fraternity bath. He wiped the sweat and filth from his body with the cool, wet cloth. It was Nirvana. Alfardaws. Glathsheim. A slice of pure heaven.

In the middle of his ablution the buzzing of Birddog overhead signaled a transmission. He reached for his radio and punched the button. "Birddog from Bat Twenty-one. Why does the phone always ring when you're taking a bath?"

"Hey, Bat! You sound in good spirits. Found the bar?"

"Affirmative, Birddog. Nothing like several good belts to lubricate a man's spirits."

"Outstanding. Don't think we have enough time before daylight to play another hole. How about digging in there for the day?"

"Roger. May never leave."

Birddog chuckled. "Man, it's good to hear you feeling better. We'll finish the ninth tomorrow and start the back nine." There was a pause, then, "We're gonna make it, Bat."

"Never doubted it," Hambleton lied.

"Sleep tight. Birddog out."

"Good night, Birddog."

Hambleton finished his bath and dressed. Then he took his knife and quietly hacked off a dozen large banana leaves. With half of them he made himself a nest on the ground near a large banana plant. Then he crawled in and pulled the remaining fronds over on top of him. When he had arranged his comforter, not even his nose stuck out. If anyone found him during the day, it would be because they stepped on him.

As he relaxed, a fleeting thought crossed his mind. He shut his eyes, his body tensing. Banana plants were often the habitat of scorpions, spiders and centipedes. He could be sharing his home with any number of antisocial insects. Then he grunted and sighed. What the hell. If they didn't like him, they could damn well leave.

Very quickly after that a tidal wave of total fatigue rolled over him. Soon he was spinning down and down. And then came oblivion, the very depths of sleep.

The Tenth Day

Campbell walked into the BOQ bathroom where Dennis Clark was taking a shower.

Clark wiped the soap out of one eye, pulled back the shower curtain, and peeked out. "What say, moneybags?"

"You just get up?"

"Roger."

Clark stepped out and grabbed a towel. "Nothing like a hot shower to put the world back on an even keel. Wish to hell I could wrap one up and drop it to Hambleton. After ten days, God, what he probably wouldn't give for a hot bath!"

Must be getting pretty ripe. How's he doing, roomie?"

"Holding in there. Holed in on the eight green. At least he's got water. Spirits were pretty good early this morning."

"Gotta hand it to that old boy. But it's not the best deal for a senior citizen."

"No, nor for a junior citizen. We haven't been able to yank Lieutenant Clark out, either. Gooks are gettin' downright nasty."

"How come it's taken so long? Thought the SAR types grabbed up shot-down aircrews before their chutes hit the ground."

"Not Air Rescue's fault. They're itching to go in again. But the Commies have attacked on four fronts. For your information, moneybags, this is a balls-out invasion. The nastys decided on a quick, massive attack to crush the South Vietnamese before they can develop their military machine. Believe me, the Commies are loaded for bear. They ain't kidding around."

"Well, from where this peace monger sits, I'd say the black hats are succeeding."

"At this point yes. They're putting on the pressure, *HARD*. It's never taken this long to yank out a downed airman. I think both Hambleton and Clark are setting some kind of record for time on the ground. It's been ten days now for Hambleton, and the Air-Rescue gents are having a coronary. They don't like it. They've pulled out a couple thousand downed fliers in this brouhaha already. Sometimes I think the SAR gents have the only mission in this fouled-up war that makes any sense."

"You're not forgetting the finance officer."

"No. I'm not forgetting the finance officer."

Campbell flopped down on the bed and stretched out. "So what else do you think would make sense?"

"All I'm saying is take off the shackles and let us do the job right."

"What shackles?"

"Case in point." Clark pulled on his flying boots. "Just last week one of our Thud pilots was on patrol. He saw a couple gook tanks heading south, so he peeled off and went down after them. Went through a lot of flak, but shot them up pretty good. He landed back at his base, expecting at least one atta-boy for a job well done. What did he get? He got a one-hundred-and-fifty-dollar fine for violating FAA regulations because he strayed from an air corridor."

"You're kidding."

Clark raised his right hand. "As God is my witness! Here we are, fighting an all-out enemy offensive. They're coming down in droves, rolling over the poor damned South Vietnamese, throwing everything at us but the kitchen sink. One of our throttle jocks goes in to help, and he's fined by the FAA for his trouble. *Our* FAA! Now does that sort of give you a clue about how we're fighting this war?"

"All right, already. I'm with you, roomie. But in the final analysis, has there ever been a war that was really intelligent?"

Clark rose and put on his survival vest. "Hell, no. All wars should be outlawed. But all I'm saying is, if war is inevitable and we *are* committed, let's go in full bore and stamp out the fire. Not just fan the flames. If it's stupid for a country to commit itself to war, then it's the height of stupidity, once committed, not to win it."

"I must remember that."

"You do that." Clark checked his .38, holstered it, and picked up his helmet. "In the meantime, I've got a date with a nice old duck who's a victim of your cruddy war." He picked up his flight bag. As he headed for the door, the phone rang. Campbell answered it, then held it toward Clark.

Clark crossed to the phone, picked it up.

"Clark, Colonel Walker. Glad I got you before you took off. Can you come to the command post on your way to the flight line?"

"Yes, sir. Problems?"

"Problems. An intelligence report. Brief you on it when you get here."

"Yes, sir. On my way."

"A sticky wicket?" asked Campbell.

"A problem. Don't know how bad. I'll find out at the CP."

The command post was a flurry of excitement. Operations orders and contingency plans were being worked on in preparation for the much-discussed blockade, in the event the President now decided to impose it.

Clark walked over to a harried Colonel Walker. As he approached, Walker gave him a glance and said, "Be right with you, Clark." Clark nodded and leaned against a desk while Walker concluded a conference with several staff officers. Then Walker motioned for the FAC pilot. "Clark, we just got some photos taken of a reconnaissance drone that flew over Hambleton's area. The intelligence types have spotted half a dozen armored personnel carriers in it. Their guess is that the Charleys have made it through the mine field, searched for Hambleton, and found him missing. That's why they've brought in the additional troops. They probably plan to make a fan-out search. It's going to get very hairy. So the sooner we can get him to the river, the better."

"Very well, sir. I'll get him started as soon as it's dark."

"You have to. I know he's just about had it, and it's going to be tough pushing him like this. But it's our only chance."

"One question, Colonel. All of this planning for the executive order? There's no chance that Colonel Hambleton's rescue will sort of get lost in the shuffle? Take a backseat?"

"Clark, that's a stupid question. I think you know our priorities."

"I'm glad that's a stupid question, sir. But I had to ask it to find out."

"We're going to recover those two men if I have to go AWOL and go in and get them personally."

"Kind of talk I like to hear."

"But we are going to be committing a lot of men and equipment if the blockade goes into effect. The staff's going to be working around the clock, so the sooner we get Hambleton and Clark out of there, the better."

"Now aren't you glad I stuck around? Nice to have an extra hand at harvest time."

"I'll be grateful to you if you just saddle up and get your ass into the blue."

"Yes, sir. On my way. Just one last thought. All this planning and midnight-oil burning is purely academic. The war will soon be over."

"That's nice to know. How do you figure?"

"I just heard that Jane Fonda's going to North Vietnam. You know she'll soon have this whole sordid mess straightened out."

"*Out!*"

"Yes, sir."

It was slow going through the banana grove as Hambleton traversed the first half of his ninth hole. Checking his compass, he could see that he would soon be out of the small plantation and into a heavy undergrowth. At least he would have protection on this hole. And it was a good thing; his problems had been underscored by the sound of voices in the distance. Had they picked up his trail? Entirely possible.

Ah, there was the edge of the grove just up ahead. Another hundred yards and he should be on the green. He paused at the last banana plant to rest and assess the terrain in front of him. It looked quiet. The only drawback was a narrow road separating him from the undergrowth. Probably used to harvest the bananas. He would have to move quickly across that bare area.

He took a deep breath and leaped. The next thing he knew, he was flipping end over end.

He landed with an agonizing grunt. He blinked the stars from his eyes and looked around. A barbed-wire fence was the culprit. Missing it in the dark, he had tripped over it, going tailbone over appetite. He swore, replaced his glasses—which were riding side-saddle on his face—and crawled over to the protection of the grove line.

He frisked himself, checking for injuries. Lucky he had hit on his head, or he might have hurt something. He checked the pocket for his radio, and then a terrible fear surged through him. His radio! It was gone! It had popped out of his pocket during the fall. Oh, dear God, not the radio! Not his only link to his rescuers; not his only hope for survival!

Frantically he fell to his knees and started searching the ground around him. Hindered by the darkness, he dug around in the fallen banana leaves, wildly pawing the ground. The coppery taste of terror began to sour his mouth. He grubbed around, skinning his hands on the rough ground, straining to see, straining to find it in the darkness.

Then he stopped abruptly in his tracks. Not panic again. Once was too much! He'd play it cozy, just sit down, relax, and think. Radio had to be around somewhere. Bouncing around like a spastic jumping jack, making lots of noise, would draw the gomers.

He sat down on his haunches, taking deep breaths. Then the moon flashed through a passing cloud long enough to throw back a dim reflection. It was the antenna. The radio was out in the middle of the narrow road. He exhaled, murmuring a short prayer of thanks.

His feeling of gratitude was quickly replaced by a sickening thought: What if the radio had been broken when he flipped and it hit the ground? It was sturdy, but not built to withstand this kind of treatment.

He looked around, listening for any signs of activity. There were still voices in the distance. Were they sounding a little closer? As far as he could see ahead and up and down the road, there was nothing but stillness. He had to cross that road to continue the hole anyway. He would make a dash for it and pick up the radio on the run.

He tensed unwilling muscles and leaped. In a flash he was across the road, the radio in his hand. Quickly he slipped into the undergrowth that bordered the far side of the road and squatted down. He waited for his heart to stop thumping as he listened again for any signs of detection. None.

His hands shaking, he turned the radio over in his palms. Examining more by feel than by sight, he determined that the hard casing was undamaged. But was it still working on the inside? He had to call Birddog and find out. He punched the transmitter button and whispered into the mike. "Birddog from Bat Twenty-one. Birddog from Bat Twenty-one. Come in."

He sat down, wiped the sweat from his brow and waited. Ten

seconds. Twenty seconds. Was he transmitting? Or was he transmitting but something had happened to the receiver? "Birddog, this is Bat Twenty-one. Come in. *Please!*"

No response. Birddog always responded immediately whenever he was in the air. Something *had* to be wrong with his radio. He fiddled with the small telescopic antenna. It appeared to be OK. He rechanneled the selector. It seemed to be working. He banged the case several times against the palm of his hand. Sweat was now pouring down his cheeks and dripping off his chin. He'd try another channel. Maybe it was just the discrete frequency that wasn't working. He punched Guard channel and called again. "Birddog from Bat Twenty-one. Do you read on Guard channel?"

"Bat Twenty-one, this is Birddog. Get the hell off Guard frequency!"

Hambleton slumped with relief. Never in his whole life had a voice sounded so good. He rechanneled to Charlie channel. "Roger, Birddog. Testing my radio. I fell. Thought I might have broken something."

"Coming in loud and clear, Bat. You caught me pouring a cup of coffee."

"Would you make that two? With a large brandy on the side. I got the shivering fits."

"Later, Bat. Right now you gotta get moving. How's your progress?"

"Calculate another hundred yards to the green."

"Then use your five iron. Get there in a hurry. You got foursomes behind you. Carrying large clubs."

"Understand." So he was right. Those were searchers he had heard talking to one another, beating the brush. "I'll shoot now."

"Roger, Bat. Check in at the green."

"Wilco."

Again Hambleton started off. The dense undergrowth was a mixed blessing. It offered good protection, but it was slow and tough going, hard to stay on the fairway. He stopped often, checking his compass, counting his paces.

In his physical state, it took him nearly an hour to cover the yardage that should have positioned the ninth-hole green. As he counted off his last stride, he stopped and looked around. He was at the east edge of the undergrowth. There was a large tree nearby. He inched over to it slowly and sat down.

It was difficult to bring his tired eyes into focus. He took off his glasses, cleaned them with his handkerchief, and replaced them. Either his eyes were playing tricks on him or his thinking had turned fuzzy. It looked like a big sandbar out there just past the border of the undergrowth. He stared at it intently, trying to make sense out of the big light place that might be a rice paddy, yet wasn't a rice paddy. It looked more like sand. He cursed himself for not being able to bring it in more clearly.

Maybe if he lay down, shut his eyes, and relaxed a minute, his fatigued brain would register a better impression. He did. Lying on his stomach, he closed his eyes for a moment, then opened them. It was coming in a little clearer. Then the moonlight broke through for a brief instant; he slowly raised on one elbow, then up on his hands and knees and muttered softly. What an idiot he was! That wasn't a paddy, that was the river, the by-God, ever-lovin' river!

He rose to his feet and stood, back to the tree, just staring at it.

And then he committed a grave tactical error. Without thinking he began to move as rapidly as he could toward the beckoning Lorelei of the water. On he blundered, faster and faster, his head bent forward like a charging bull. And suddenly his left foot came down where there wasn't any ground.

In survival school he had been warned of the abrupt drop-offs and cliffs in this part of the country. But when he saw the water before him, his mind had donned blinders. In an instant he was rolling, tumbling, bouncing down a steep embankment. Too late to prevent him from stepping into midair, his survival training at least prompted him to clasp his arms around his head, buffering his fall as he logrolled down the cliff.

He banged to a painful stop against a tree.

His wind knocked out of him, he fought dizziness. Don't go under now, Hambone. Just because you're stupid enough to walk off a cliff, don't go under now. It could be fatal. He lay there stunned for several minutes. Feeling more outrage for his stupidity than actual pain from the fall, he cursed himself unmercifully.

Gingerly he tested his extremities: his fingers, hands, then arms and legs. Although reluctantly, everything seemed to respond. Finally he rolled over on his stomach and his eyes fell on the river. He was seeing it, but not quite believing it. Only one way to find out. Ignoring the pain from his fall, like a snake he wriggled on his belly down to the river's edge and put his hands into the dark water. It was no mirage. In spite of his stupidity, he had achieved his objective. With perfect sincerity he said, "Thank you, sweet Jesus. Thank you."

He immersed his face in the water and took a long drink. Polluted or not, it tasted delicious. He took another drink, then rolled over on his back. A feeling of exhilaration swept through him. He had finished the front nine of his golf game. Rescue would now be just around the corner. He had to share his good news with the FAC; Birddog would be delighted to know he had reached the Suwannee.

He crawled back up the bank to the shelter of the tree that had stopped his fall, and pulled out his radio. Wonder of wonders, the radio had survived another calamity intact. If nothing else, this war had proved that the good ole USA sure as hell made rugged radios. Or were they made in Japan?

"Congratulations, Bat. Keep up this score and you'll win the tournament. How do you feel?"

"Bushed. But happy."

"Outstanding. How you doing physically?"

"Bring on Joe Louis." He didn't expect Birddog to believe that, but what was the point of telling the truth? He was bone tired, and the fall down the cliff sure as hell hadn't built him up any. His shoulder was acting funny—not the one with the knife hole in it, the other one. But damned if he was going to complain now.

"Good. Because you're in a very hot area. Angry duffers coming your way. You gotta make like Esther Williams."

"Esther Williams?"

"Affirmative. If that doesn't ring a bell, try Johnny Weismuller."

"What do I do when I make like Esther Williams?"

"Make like Esther Williams will do when she goes to her great reward."

Damn this double-talk. What the hell would Esther Williams do when she went to her great reward? Not fall off a cliff like he had! No! Maybe step off the deep end? No, dive off maybe! No, that would solve nothing. Oh hell! "Not reading you, Birddog."

"Does the name Styx mean anything to you? Sugar, tango, Yankee, Xray?"

Styx. The river Styx. The ancient myth. You crossed the river Styx to reach the great beyond. When Esther went to her final reward she would have to cross the river Styx. Which meant he had to cross the river. Now where the hell did they dredge up that little gem? Probably it was the fine hand of Frank Ott. "Roger, Birddog. Now I read you."

"Good. You'll have to start right away. No time to lose. Can you do it?"

"I'll try."

"I got money bet on this game. Don't let me down. Check in after you've gone to your great reward."

"I don't like the way you put that. Bat Twenty-one out."

Hambleton clicked off and looked out over the river. What had looked like a godsend only moments before now looked like an impassable abyss. It didn't look more than a couple hundred feet in width, but it might as well have been the Gulf of Mexico. A curtain of doom began to eclipse his elation. He had to shake it off. Think positive, Hambone. You've performed miracles thus far. You've survived for ten days. You've walked through mine fields, skirted enemy gun crews, threaded an enemy village, fought hand-to-hand combat for your life. If young Clark can do it, you can do it. Someone up there is looking after you. No reason He should let you down now.

The distant sound of crashing brush snapped him out of his reverie. He had to come to grips with the problem at hand. If he had to swim that river he would have to strip down to bare essentials. He took a fast inventory. He would take only his radio, flares, and knife. His gun, first-aid kit, and other paraphernalia, including his survival vest, would have to stay behind.

He removed the vest, feeling almost as if he was parting with an old friend; shinnied up the bank to where he had spotted a small cave; and dropped the gear into it. He covered it with silt from the river bank, and then finally turned to face the river.

He could hear the thrashing of bushes to the north and south of him. His heart palpitating at the sight of the wide stretch of forbidding water he had to cross, he ventured out into it up to his knees. Fool! He'd forgotten something. He could not possibly swim that river with his boots and socks on. Had to start thinking straight. He returned to the bank, sat down, and removed his footgear. He hid them under an old uprooted tree, and again he cautiously eased into the water.

Wading out, the bottom suddenly dropped out from under

him as he stepped into a hole, finding himself in over his head. He came up spitting and choking, holding the radio in a vise grip above his head, trying to keep it dry.

It was going to be tough if he had to swim all the way across. The current was slow, but it was certainly no help. Twenty feet from shore he was already fighting fatigue. He had to rest.

He dropped to his feet, and to his surprise found them resting on the rocky bottom. He stood up, the water lapping at his chest. He had guessed the water to be much deeper; hell, he might be able to *walk* across. He tried walking for several yards. It was slow going, but the water did not rise above his shoulders. Then he realized he had added another tactical error to his list.

The river bottom was lined with sharp, rough rocks that cut into his bare feet. He stubbed his toe on the next step, sending a spasm of pain shooting through his body. It would be impossible to cross that river barefoot. And he was too bushed to try swimming it.

Again he turned around and headed back to shore to pick up his boots. Half swimming, half wading, he got back to the river bank. Luckily he had ditched his boots under that fallen tree, and it was a visible silhouette in the dark. He found them, sat down on the log, and pulled on wet socks. Then he pushed his feet back into the clumsy clodhoppers and zipped them up.

In spite of being wet and soggy, the rubber and nylon boots felt good on his feet. They had almost become a part of him; they were made for traveling in water and jungle environments, and he cursed himself for even thinking of parting with such old friends. Maybe he was making a mistake leaving his survival vest, too. Maybe he should go back and get it. And his gun.

Wrestling with this decision, he glimpsed a flashlight beam darting near the hedgerow he had just vacated. The decision had been made for him. He headed back into the river.

He swam over the hole in which he had foundered the first time, then let his feet down to the rocky bottom. He walked very slowly. He did not want to step into another hole and drown. And besides the slower he went the fewer ripples and less noise he made in the water. Quietly, step by step, he negotiated the slippery river bottom. He was lucky. Except for the original hole near the west bank, he did not hit any spot with water deeper than neck high.

After what seemed an eternity he reached the far bank and waded ashore. He lay for a moment, summoning strength. Then on hands and knees he crawled into the thickets that lined the bank. He was safe again—at least for the moment—but God, he was tired! It was all he could do to pull the big dark leaves of the undergrowth over him before he collapsed.

It took the impatient buzzing of Birddog to give him the strength to turn on his radio. "Come in, Birddog."

There was obvious relief in the voice of the FAC pilot. "Good to hear your voice, Bat Twenty-one. How goes it?"

"Esther Williams just went to her great reward."

"Outstanding. Ready for the back nine?"

"Sure would appreciate a short rest."

"Negative on that. Many fireflies on the course. Imperative you knock off at least one more hole."

Fireflies? Hambleton sat up and looked out of his conceal- ment. They did look like fireflies—flickering flashlights silhouet- ting figures on the west bank not far from where he had entered the river. Dear God! Would they cross the river?

"Understand, Birddog. Will tee off shortly."

"Know it's tough, Bat. But more holes will get you farther from the fireflies."

"Understand."

"On the back nine you'll have to make like Charley Tuna. Turn left and follow the Suwannee. Length of hole is very important, so we'll know where you are. We'll play the back course of Tucson National. Remember it?"

"Affirmative." Hambleton knew the yards of each hole at Tucson to the inch. Even with his fuzzy mind.

"Good. Tee off now. Check in when you reach the green of hole number ten."

"Wilco."

"Be careful, Bat."

"Thanks. Bat Twenty-one out."

So he was going to have to get back into the river, and go with it downstream. He did not relish the thought. The holes, the floundering, the slippery rocks, the constant worry about getting his radio wet. But he had to do it, and it was time to go. The more real estate he could put between himself and the gomers, the better.

Noiselessly he crept down to the river's edge. Now even the smallest movement was becoming a real chore. His tired body sent incessant pangs of protest to his frazzled brain; every exertion was the last lap of a four-minute mile. He slipped into the water and headed downstream, trying to stay near the bank where it was the shallowest, hugging the overhang. In some places the water was only knee-deep. The next instant he would be in over his head, fighting for his life, but always in deadly fear his splashing would attract the enemy. The darkness further impeded his progress, tripping him with unseen snags, slapping him with invisible branches. As he made his way he tried to keep accurate count of his yards traveled, measuring his progress as best he could in sliding, stumbling strides.

After an hour of this, Hambleton had to rest. He half staggered, half rolled up onto a grassy bank. He had only clicked off three hundred yards of his tenth hole; he still had another one hundred and twenty to go. As he lay there, deathly still, trying not to pant too loudly, he heard a splash in the water. It sounded very close. He snapped to a sitting position, his nerve ends raw. Had the enemy crossed the river? He reached for his knife and steeled himself.

And then he could make out the hump that broke the surface of the river, swimming downstream. A large mud turtle! He had startled it from its resting place and it was off to find some spot less populated. He swallowed the heart that had lodged in his throat, and sat down in the mud, trembling.

He looked back up the river. The flashlights were barely visible now, and he seemed to be out of range of the voices. Odd they had not crossed the river. Or had they? He stood up to look upstream. If there were any gomers on his side of the river they were not to be seen or heard. Maybe there was one thing going for him: The river had averaged neck high to his six-foot-two frame. That would be over the head of an average Vietnamese. If they all had to swim with their battle gear and rifles, that might be a very discouraging project.

Careful. He couldn't get carried away on a false sense of security. He might have the gomers temporarily stymied, but what they lacked in physical stature they more than compensated for in resourcefulness and guts. He hadn't seen the end of them. Now he had to get off his butt and get on downstream.

Wearily he sank back into the river, holding onto the vines at the bank's edge. His foot slipped, plunging him into a deep hole. He came up spitting muddy water and cursing. Treading water, he floated along until his feet again touched bottom. Still holding his radio up at arm's length, he started wading toward the bank.

Suddenly he felt something hit the funny bone of his elbow. The jolt sent a tingling sensation up his arm as he whipped around. He stepped back. It hit him again, this time on the chest. He could not believe his eyes as the form slowly materialized in the darkness.

It was a solid, thick railroad tie! Almost ten feet long. He reached out and touched it; it bobbed slightly under his hand. He put his arm around it. The front end submerged, so he slid it by him and tried again, this time putting his full weight on the log's midsection. Again it partly submerged, but it supported his weight.

He had a conveyance! Something on which to ride. He put his arm around it in a firm grip and floated, grasping the growth of the overhang and guiding himself along. He strode effortlessly keeping track of his clicks. By God, this was a hell of a lot easier. And the log would provide protection to hide behind in case he should be intercepted. This was living!

He examined the log as he floated toward the green of his tenth hole. A black smudge came off on his hand. Charcoal. It was charred on one end. Could it be from the bombed-out bridge upstream, the one the Air Force had clobbered? Wherever it came from, whatever its origin, it was a godsend. Providence had provided him with a golf cart. Now he was going to finish the back nine in style.

The Eleventh Day

In the command post Major Sam Piccard was briefing Colonel Frank Ott. Piccard pointed at a spot on the reconnaissance map that had the overlap of Hambleton's golf course drawn in. "He's right here, Colonel. Just got the report from Birddog—he's holed up on the eleventh green, there on the river bank."

Ott studied the map. "So ole Hambone's now tucked away eleven holes. Knowing him, he did it under par."

"According to Birddog's message, he now has a golf cart."

Ott grinned. "A golf cart?"

"So he says. We're still trying to figure that one out. He's probably found some floating debris, something to hang on to."

"Leave it to Hambleton."

Piccard struck a match to his pipe, and squinted at Ott through a swirl of blue smoke. "War's a game. Cowper said it."

Ott looked questioningly at the pockmarked face of the intelligence officer. "Cowper?"

"Eighteenth century poet. 'But war's a game, which, were their subjects wise, kings would not play at.'"

"Umm," said Ott. "You know Sam, for an intelligence officer you ain't too stupid."

Piccard grinned. "I read a lot. I used to read everything I could get my hands on dealing with war. Hoped I might be able to understand it, make some kind of sense out of it. But it's like wading in quicksand. The deeper you get into it, the worse it gets."

"That's for sure."

"Now I read to try to forget the war. Ever read Hercule Poirot?"

"James Bond man, myself."

Colonel Walker approached the two men. With him was a tall, husky Marine lieutenant colonel. Walker introduced the Marine to the two men as Colonel Andrews, commander of a Marine Ranger detachment. Going up to the map, Walker pointed out Hambleton's present position to the Marine.

"He seems to be making good time," said Andrews, "for a man who's been suffering ten days of exposure."

"Hambleton," said Ott, "was never much for throwing in the towel."

Walker addressed the Marine. "Got your men in place, Andrews?"

"Soon will be, sir. They've already started."

"It's going to be a rough mission."

"Don't forget, Colonel Walker," said Andrews, grinning, "these men are *Marines*."

Walker snorted. "Marines or no Marines, they've got a damned dangerous mission."

Sam Piccard studied the face of the Marine. "War is a tricky damned business, and messy as hell when you come right down to it. Here we are, purposely parachuting two more men into an area we're busting a gut to get one downed man out of."

"Please, Sam," Walker growled, "no more of that. Especially not from you. I get enough of it from headquarters. If Andrews here hadn't gone to bat with me topside, we'd never have gotten approval for this mission."

"No argument, Colonel."

"I'm not making many points with headquarters. Not that I don't understand their rationale—they have their reasons. They make sense. They're looking at the big picture—losses, body counts, how many green sacks to order. Understandably, they want to keep our losses down, but sometimes generals forget how it is at the fighting level. When you are a Mother Superior to a flock of fly-boys you just don't let them down. Christ Almighty! How a stinking war can put a guy's nuts in a vise! I wish to hell we'd quit having them."

Andrews tactfully cleared his throat. "Don't worry about our men going in, gentlemen. They can take care of themselves. No sweat."

Walker turned to the Marine. "There will be sweat, Andrews. Marines or no Marines, there will be sweat."

"Granted, sir. But these are Rangers. Especially trained for escape and evasion. They know their stuff. All volunteers. Hand-picked."

A tired grin tugged the corners of Walker's mouth. "That's why I've always had a soft spot in my heart for the Marines. Only branch of the services that handpicks their volunteers."

Through high cirrus clouds a waxing moon was beginning to bathe the landscape in soft shadows.

With an effort Hambleton relaxed his grip on the log. Ignore the leeches on your legs. Forget about the snakes that slither across the fairway. When would it be better to have a case of diarrhea from drinking polluted water than while floating down a river? Look at the bright side. Think upbeat. Five more holes and you'll be finished. Uncle Sam's paying you just to play golf. Only the big pros get paid for playing golf.

His eyes closed. When he opened them again he was not surprised to see Gwen sitting on the front of the log, pert as a peony, wearing her sexy new yellow bathing suit. God, she did look lovely in the moonlight. And desirable.

As he reached out his hand, she dissolved into the charcoaled end of the railroad tie. He shook his head and wiped his eyes. Got to knock it off! Got to stop these hallucinations. Second time tonight.

He splashed some water on his face. Three hundred and sixty-five, three hundred and sixty-six, three hundred and sixty-seven ...

He stared vacuously ahead, silently floating on the lazy current, his legs moving in slow, rhythmic strides, his feet some-times touching bottom—sometimes not—as he subconsciously counted the yards to the green. Three hundred and eighty. There. A tiny flag went up in his brain. Three hundred and eighty yards. This should be the end of the fourteenth hole, a little grassy spot up ahead.

Grasping the bushes of the overhang, he maneuvered himself and his log over to the bank. Then, pulling and shoving with what little strength he could marshal, he finally got the log far enough up on the bank to secure it. Then he covered it with branches from the overhang, clucking over it like it really was a ten-thousand-dollar golf cart. Maybe it didn't have a wet bar, stereo, and color television like Bob Hope's, but it had something else. It was here and it just might be responsible for saving his life.

The energy spent in covering his tracks left him weak. He crawled a few yards away and disappeared into the undergrowth. He had to rest. He would take a thirty-minute nap, then check in with Birddog.

He stretched out on his back, trying to get comfortable. It was difficult to do; his shoulder was giving him a bad time. It had been acting up ever since his roll down the cliff, and now it was getting worse. He squirmed down into the brush, nesting, favoring his shoulder.

A prickling sensation in his leg brought him back into a sitting position. He had almost forgotten. His hands flew to his ankles, and he zipped open the left leg of his flying suit. There it was. His skin crawled with revulsion. A fat leech had attached itself to his lower calf. Its small sawlike teeth were making the incision in his flesh. Through this it would soon draw the blood for its ugly, sucking mouth. Goddamn, how he hated the miserable, slimy things.

Grimacing, he picked the loathsome creature off his flesh, pulling hard before the flat mouth finally released its suction. With an oath he flung it far away into the bushes. He squeezed the wound making the blood rinse out the hole. As if he had any blood to spare—that free-lunching obscenity! He shuddered. How in hell had Humphrey Bogart ever gotten the *African Queen* down that river? Of all the things in the jungle, he despised leeches most, more even than the great snakes that slithered along the riverbank, and the mind-shattering clouds of ravenous mosquitoes.

He cleaned the wound as best he could with his handkerchief, and zipped up his pants leg. Too bad he couldn't have brought his first-aid kit; at least he could stem the infection. He leaned back again, endeavoring to get comfortable. He tried not to think of his physical condition. Slowly but surely he was becoming one hell of a mess. He would make a great training aid for a medical school. Some of his little flak wounds were festering on various parts of his body. His finger, thank God, was knitting. The stab wound in his shoulder didn't bother him too much either. But his other shoulder nagged like hell.

Not that any of it was able to compete for his attention very often against the cramps in his stomach. It had not been too wise to fill his empty gut with river water. The diarrhea now almost doubled him up at times.

Four holes. Could he make it? Doubt again invaded his mind. Could he possibly make four more holes? Over fifteen hundred yards? Didn't sound like much—not even a mile. But when each step took a concerted effort of will, when each movement required an agonized appraisal, it might as well be from here to the moon. If he had any sense at all he would just roll over right now and cash it in. Find respite from his misery. He closed his eyes and tried to push the crazy thoughts from his brain.

After a moment his lids flicked open. What was that? He had heard something. There it was again, coming from the river. A splashing. Sound really carried along the stretch of water. He recognized the noise and cautiously rose to a sitting position. It was a paddle splashing, no mistake.

He leaned forward until he could peer through the brush. Then he felt the hairs on the back of his neck rise. Fifty yards upstream was a sampan.

He sucked in his breath and held it. Luck was not with him. There were no clouds to block the moon, and in its eerie light he could see the large eyeball painted on the prow of the sampan. It came closer, like some weird, silent monster from the depths. As it approached he could make out half a dozen soldiers sitting in the longboat, facing both sides of the river, their guns resting in their laps. Now and then beams from flashlights flicked out, exploring the banks.

Closer it came, the oarsmen stationed at the prow and the stern quietly propelling the boat with synchronized dips of their paddles. Would they see his log, pulled partway up on the bank? A railroad tie would look out of place on the banks of a Vietnamese river, and it was bound to raise suspicion.

The sampan was now abreast of him. His heart stopped as he saw the beam of a flashlight fall upon his log. One of the soldiers in the prow of the boat said something in a low voice, and pointed at the railroad tie with his rifle. The oarsman in the prow brought the boat around, aiming its bow directly at the log. Hambleton froze, not daring to breathe as the sampan nosed toward the bank. Dear God, were they going to get out? Search the place? Instinctively he reached for his knife.

The paddler punched the railroad tie with his oar as the soldiers in the boat watched. More flashlights flicked on, and Hambleton recoiled into his hiding place as the beams swept the undergrowth around him. As the fingers of light probed the darkness, an eternity limped by.

The oarsman in the prow stepped out of the boat and waded over to examine the log with his flashlight. He swept the beam up and down its length, then reached down to touch the charred end. He brought back his hand, examining it. Seeing the charred black on his fingers, he went back to the boat and said something to the soldiers. Hambleton could see him pointing upstream, in the direction of the bombed-out bridge. There were several more words in whispered Vietnamese, then the oarsman made one last sweep of the underbrush with his flashlight. He shoved the beached boat off the bank, jumped in, and resumed his position in the prow.

The sampan continued downstream like a ghostly spectre, its paddles quietly dipping into the water.

Hambleton exhaled. He was a dishrag. He lay back, collapsing. He closed his eyes as his morale yo-yo hit the bottom of its string, broke, and went spinning off into the river.

Dawn was just touching the sky when Captain Clark set the wheels of his O-2 onto the landing strip. He automatically went through the abbreviated postlanding checklist as he taxied to his revetment on the flight line. He spun the little plane around and chopped the power. Making a quick notation in the plane's Form 781, he climbed out, stretching the stiffness from his body. Then he noticed a tall, lone figure ambling up to him.

"Morning, Clark."

Clark recognized Hambleton's old friend. "Good morning, Colonel Ott. You're up very early. Or very late."

"Ain't it the truth. I know you've been flying all night and are ready to hit the sack. But I thought I might help you unwind with a cup of coffee first."

"You're on. How about we patronize the exclusive flight-line lounge? There's always a hot pot brewing there. Hydraulic fluid, but it's hot."

"Good. Just want to chat a minute."

Clark picked up his flight bag and threw his parachute over his shoulder. In silence the two men walked the short distance to the maintenance shack. Clark threw his gear into a chair and drew coffee from the urn. Then, sitting himself on the decrepit divan, he hiked his cowboy boots up on the coffee table.

"So, Colonel, what do we chat about."

"It's Hambleton. I wanted to get the latest, firsthand."

"Our friend Hambleton just crawled into the sixteenth hole. And I mean crawled."

"That bad?"

"That bad. Frankly, Colonel, I'm worried. Very worried. Naturally his physical condition has been deteriorating bit by bit. But his stamina's way down and for the first time I think his rationality is beginning to slip. The old fire has gone out of his voice. Some of his messages are incoherent—have to be repeated. And tonight he had a real scare. Some gooks cruising in a sampan stopped not ten yards away and inspected his golf cart."

"So they have taken to the river, have they?"

"It appears that way. And it raises a helluva lot of problems."

"Did you see any on your cap last night?"

"No. But that doesn't mean they aren't there. When they hear my plane they must just pull over near the bank. Impossible to spot them under all that vegetation. If they could be spotted, we'd bring in the Sandys."

"How about bringing in the Specters? The C-130's could drop flares and light up the place."

Clark shook his head. "Thought of that too. No dice. Hambleton has to travel at night. Lighting up the river would expose the gooks, but it would also expose him. We'd defeat our purpose."

"See what you mean."

"That could be a lone sampan he saw, or there could be a dozen cruising the river. No way of knowing."

"Did Ham see any others besides the one that pulled up by his log?"

"That's all he reported."

"Then we are dealing with an unknown. He's still got six hundred yards to go to the eighteenth hole. And you say he's crawling."

"He's crawling. Takes him longer and longer between holes.

He had to rest two hours before he had the strength to tackle the last one. To be honest, I don't know how the hell he's hung on this long. Eleven days with a couple ears of corn. I miss one meal and I think I'm going to die. And he's been forced to drink the river water. Jesus! That river's a sewer."

"Hambleton has a strong will to survive. He's got a lot to live for. If anyone can pull through, he will."

"That's what I keep telling him. But damn, it's getting tough. Being up there with him night after night, listening to his voice, always trying to be cheerful, knowing damned well the hell he's going through. And there's not a damned thing I can really do to help him."

"You've done plenty, Clark. A man couldn't ask for a better guardian angel."

"Hell of a guardian angel! Sitting around on my keester while a beat-up old geezer twice my age drags himself through the mud by his teeth not fifty feet below my airplane."

"Don't blame yourself. No man could do more."

"Got to do more. For starters, I'm going to see if we can't try another air drop. If we could sanitize the area around him with Sandys, then maybe we could get a drop to him that he could reach. Some food and water just might get him off his knees and on to the last two holes."

Ott thought for a moment. "A calculated risk. A drop would certainly pinpoint him. And since the enemy is searching the area..."

"I've been thinking about that. One drop would pinpoint. But how about a dozen drops?"

Ott's brows puckered. "A dozen drops?"

"Twelve. We'll make twelve drops. All will be dummies but one. The one we'll drop over Hambleton will have a CARE package. We'll spread the others all around the area. With a dozen chutes opening all across the sky, the gooks will be running around in circles."

Ott nodded. "Not a bad idea. An element of risk, but not a bad idea."

"I think the element of risk is acceptable if it will get food, water, first aid—and cigarettes—to him. It just might be enough to help get our old navigator through."

"Very well. While you hit the sack I'll run your idea by Colonel Walker."

"I'd appreciate it, sir. Best time to drop will be around dusk, while it's still light enough for Hambleton to spot it, yet getting dark so he can retrieve it."

"First rate. Good thinking, Clark."

Clark looked at Ott. There was something about the man he had liked right from their first meeting. "Just routine. Doesn't compare with that eighteen-hole caper you came up with."

"Huh! If it works. But I can't take the credit. A lot of input went into that one. When we sent the word out for Ham's old golfing buddies, you should have seen the duffers crawl out of the woodwork begging to help. All over the world. There was even a master sergeant who checked in from Australia. Said he used to be Hambleton's caddy. With that kind of response it was no trick to line up the holes we knew Hambone would be familiar with."

"Don't sell yourself short. It was a hell of an idea."

"Let's not break an arm patting anyone on the back until we've got our golfer safely in the clubhouse."

Clark nodded. "When it comes right down to it, it's not a bad outfit, is it?"

"What's not a bad outfit?"

"The blooming Air Force."

"No. Not bad. At least it tries to take care of its own."

Clark looked at the colonel. "Tell me, you're an old friend of Hambleton's. I've spent a week and a half with the guy, through hell and high water. But I've never met the man. What's he like?"

"You mean that you've never even seen him?"

"No."

"Well, to answer your question—physically he's not much out of the ordinary. A tall, lanky drink of cactus juice. Has a tanned, lined face. Ham always looked to me like he'd be more at home driving a farm tractor than navigating a sophisticated flying machine. Has the look of a farmer."

"So he's not your typical, handsome Air Force type—like me?"

"Handsome?" Ott chuckled. "You'd hardly call Ham handsome. But inside, that's where the old duffer shines. He's an honest, warm, sensitive, intelligent guy with a nice, martini-dry sense of humor. A man's man, I guess, but women like him too. I don't know many men who've known Hambleton who wouldn't rate him in the top box. Does that answer your question?"

"It helps. But the description you gave hardly conjures the hero image."

"The *hero* image?"

"Affirmative. Win or lose, alive or posthumously, Hambleton will come out of this fracas a highly decorated man. He ignored his personal safety to transmit enemy movements, and caused the destruction of a hell of a lot of gook hardware. Calling off SAM launches to our aircraft certainly saved some crew members. Just last night the fighters pickle-buttoned three SAM sites that had been dug in and weren't visible in our reccy photos. Hambleton had reported them when he was almost too weak to talk. In my book, Colonel, that's a son-of-a-bitchin' hero."

Ott grunted. "You're right. Odd, isn't it? Hambleton would be the last guy in the world to ever consider himself a hero." He scanned the face of the young pilot. "I've told you a bit about Hambleton. Now would you return the favor?"

"If I can."

"You can. Tell me about yourself. You. Captain Dennis Clark."

Clark grinned. "We can't be that hard up for conversation."

"Not conversation. Information. I'd like to know why you're doing this. Every man in this theater is counting the hours until he can go home—escape this lunatic asylum. You've finished your tour, got your orders, yet here you are volunteering to risk your butt every night for someone you don't even know. Why?"

Clark picked up his coffee cup and stood. "Another cup of Drano, Colonel?"

"No thanks. Go ahead."

Clark went to the coffee urn and came back with a filled cup. "If we ever run out of napalm, we can drop this on the women and children."

"How about answering my question?"

"Your question."

"You trying to be some kind of hero too, Clark?"

Clark shot him a cold look. "A hero, Colonel? Horse hockey!"

"Then what?"

Clark lit another cigarette. "To be honest, I don't know. My roommate says I got some kind of hang-up about my father. Campbell is sort of a Freudian fruitcake. He majored in psychology at college, and every time I lie down he tries to analyze me."

"What about your father?"

"My father's dead. Cancer."

"I'm sorry."

"No sweat."

"How did you get along with him?"

Clark smiled. "You're beginning to sound like my roommate. My father and I got along great until I started college. Then things sorta came unglued. I got all involved in a campus radical group, smoked pot, fooled around with drugs, became an activist in the antiwar movement, finally got kicked out of school and blew a four-year scholarship. Naturally I had a falling-out with my parents."

"Not exactly atypical."

"Yeah. I wasn't exactly alone. But I came home one night to get my clothes. I was going to live in a commune with my girl friend. Dad and I had a scene. To show you what class I had, I ended up spitting in his face. He never spoke to me again. Died a week later."

"I see."

"A thing like that can shake a young troop up. It really jerked my head around. I did an about-face, joined the Air Force, and became a pilot."

"I assume Campbell has it all figured out. Hambleton has replaced your father, and subconsciously you're trying to atone for your sins by helping the old duffer out now. That about it?"

"Pretty close."

"Do you think there's anything to it?"

Clark shrugged. "Hell, to be perfectly honest, I don't know. When Campbell first mentioned his theory, I threw him in the shower. I'd never even thought you had to have a reason for helping somebody out. As far as Hambleton was concerned, we had a problem. Hambleton was on third. I was up at bat. What's so unusual about making a little sacrifice to bring a man home?"

"Nothing."

"I don't think so either. That's why I don't understand why everybody's making such a big deal out of it."

"No big deal. It's just that these days, when antiheroes are so popular, I guess people tend to get suspicious of anyone who's distinguishing himself."

"Hell's fire, I'm just doing the job I was trained to do. Isn't that what the Air Force is all about?"

"I like to think so."

"Then why does it matter what a person's motives are? Maybe I just like doing my job. Does it really matter as long as the job gets done?"

"No. It doesn't matter."

Clark snuffed out his cigarette and looked at his watch. "Campbell should be out of the room by now. If you'll excuse me, Colonel, I'll go log some shut-eye. Get ready for tonight's mission."

"Clark, may I say just one more thing? To terminate our little chat?"

"Be my guest."

"A man's motives, like a funny joke, should never be dissected. You end up with a handful of smoke. But I know damn well there's an old bull stuck down there in the mud who's mighty thankful for your performance. Regardless of how or why it's motivated. And I wouldn't be surprised if there was a gent named Clark orbiting around upstairs somewhere who's mighty damn proud of his son."

Clark grinned at the colonel. "May I add one word to that?"

"Shoot."

"Bullshit."

It was dusk. The molten gold of the sun was gilding the horizon. Hambleton took off his mosquito netting and stuffed it into the pocket of his flying suit. It took a supreme effort to activate his sleeping bones and muscles and unite them in the common cause to sit up. He poked his head out of the bushes and scanned the river. Except for the buzzing of insects and a nearby croaking of a bullfrog, all was quiet.

The Sandy should be coming along any minute now with the CARE package. He had had mixed feelings when the FAC pilot told him they were going to try another drop. It would sure as hell give away his position. But he hadn't had the strength to argue. If it came, fine. But it would have to fall right on top of him or he wouldn't have the energy to retrieve it. And if it fell on top of him, it would be followed by a platoon of gomers. But it didn't really matter. He didn't feel as if he had a chance in hell of making another two holes anyway.

Nevertheless, he found his interest mounting as the drone of an airplane started reverberating across the river. He mounted trembling legs and stood in the shadows of a tree to watch. There were *three* airplanes coming out of the sun, low.

My Lord, it took a lot of machinery to drop one CARE package. Then he saw the drop, the nylon-bud blossoming out on down the river. Christ on a crutch! The canister was dropping way the hell and gone beyond him. He could barely see it, let alone retrieve it. What happened? Birddog knew precisely where he was; he had made a triangulation from his radio beeps before he had dug in for the day. It wasn't like the Sandy pilots to—hold it! Another chute! It was dropping at least half a click west of the river. And—holy Toledo—another one. And *another!* What the hell was going on? Must be a dozen chutes billowing all over the sky—but not one anywhere near reach. The planes disappeared as Hambleton scratched his head in wonderment. Well, so much for the resupply mission.

Suddenly there was an ear-rattling roar as a lone plane blasted up from the hill directly behind him. The pilot came in so low Hambleton instinctively ducked as the plane thundered overhead. Then he spotted the silver canister swinging from the chute. It was on a trajectory directly toward him.

So that was it! The old dazzle-'em-with-footwork ploy. They were using the other chutes as red herrings to confuse the enemy. God love 'em! He shot the disappearing plane a clenched-fist salute as it droned out of sight, rocking its wings.

The canister floated over his head toward the top of a small hill behind him, ripped a big leaf from a banana tree and disappeared from sight. It shouldn't be too hard to find. It was still too light to climb the hill, but as soon as the sun disappeared he would try.

The thought of that package up there was almost unbearable. Before half an hour had passed, he convinced himself there was enough heavy coverage on the hillside. He could keep hidden as he traveled up for it. Besides, he couldn't wait longer. It would soon be night and he would have to get back to the river and move on.

He studied the best course to take up the small hill, then he set out. Pulling the weight of his body inch by inch, he started the ascent. It was a small but steep incline. Crawling on his hands and knees, grabbing bushes and undergrowth, he pulled himself along with all his strength. Nearly halfway up, one bush he grabbed came out with its roots, and he went sliding, rolling back down the incline. Again he tried. Again he almost reached the top, actually glimpsing the chute. Then a rock let go under his footing, sending him again sprawling, crashing down through the underbrush.

Three times he tried it, but always the slope proved to be a rampart he could not conquer. Three times he slid and tumbled back to level ground. It had taken an hour of perseverance, but he had no choice but to give up. He had too little energy despite his determination; willpower was not enough. There was nothing to do but drag himself back to his hole.

He lay there panting, staring unbelieving at the top of the small knoll. What was he to do? The little hill might as well be Mount Everest. That earthen clump held his sustenance; the cornucopia that could provide fresh water, food, energy—possibly even life itself.

If he had been fit he could have figured out some way to get that canister. But he was not fit. Clear thinking, inspiration, and physical stamina had abandoned him. His only companions now were fatigue and pain. It was all he could do to plant one foot ahead of the other, let alone scale that hill. And if there were any gomers in the immediate area they would be coming in after the canister.

He closed his eyes. What should he do? What *could* he do? Had the last ray of hope just been extinguished? Crazy, irrational thoughts entered his head. Why should he prolong this agony? Why must he endure this pain and suffering any longer when there was no chance, no chance at all, of survival? Why should he keep flailing away at insurmountable odds, endangering equipment and the lives of men bent on rescuing him? Why subject any crazy, brave FAC pilot to more of this? There was no reason. No further reason.

"Birddog to Bat Twenty-one. You there, Bat? Over."

Birddog sounded relieved when he acknowledged the call. It had been a good two hours with no contact.

"No luck," said Hambleton. "Could not retrieve."

Birddog's voice went flat. "Son of a bitch!"

"Shall I stay and try again tomorrow?"

"Negative, Bat. Natives are restless. There's a large village on the other side of that hill. You have to get back into the Suwannee."

"Now?"

"Right now."

Hambleton sagged. He didn't think he could move. Yet there was no choice. He had to get the hell out of there. "Roger, Birddog."

"One thing more, Bat. A bit of good news that might help. Your buddy is now in the clubhouse."

Hambleton had to think on this for a moment before the meaning came through. "You've recovered the observer? Clark?"

"Affirmative. He's safe and sound."

"Thank God."

"You're next. Now get cracking. Birddog out."

Hambleton signed off. So they had yanked young Lieutenant Clark out. Somehow they had snagged the observer out of enemy territory. The best news he had heard since being shot down. He said a silent prayer of thanks. Maybe there was hope for him too. He felt renewed. Time to get up off the knuckles. He had heard the man. Time to get cracking!

He dragged himself down to the bank where his log lay half buried in the mud. He laboriously launched it, waded with it out into the river. He hooked his arm around the tie and started off for the seventeenth hole, more dead than alive, but now motivated by a tiny glow of new hope.

The Twelfth Day

In the Joint Chiefs of Staff Pentagon briefing room Admiral Moorer rose and examined the wall map with the overlay of Hambleton's golf course. He studied it silently for a moment, then tapped the map and turned to the briefing intelligence officer. "So he made it to the green of the seventeenth? Right here?"

"Yes, sir," replied the intelligence officer. "He should be starting the last hole shortly."

"How is his condition?"

"Very weak, sir. He was unable to recover the supply canister that was dropped to him."

"Tough break." Moorer returned to his chair. "Gentlemen, it's going to be close. Maybe our golfer's not going to make it to the eighteenth. But I want that man pulled out of there. If we have to steam up that river with the U.S.S. *Enterprise,* I want that man recovered."

There was a silent nodding of heads as Moorer turned to the Air Force Chief of Staff. "John, if Hambleton makes it, I think we should let the public affairs people run with this one. What do you think?"

"I agree," said Ryan. "We've laid an awful lot of bad news on the American people since the Communists started this invasion. I certainly think they're entitled to what little good news comes out of it. And if Hambleton makes it, it's quite a story. But we should keep a security lid on his method of escape and evasion. Just in case we might need to use it again."

"Agreed. Now gentlemen, we owe this navigator a large debt. I know sometimes we think we've got it pretty rough. We get caught between the Pentagon, the National Security Council, the Hill, and the White House. It's a full-time job just trying to hang onto sanity. We all tend to get feeling real sorry for ourselves. But we have it easy when you think about that poor guy down there in that mess and what he's been going through the last eleven days. Compared to him I realize we've got no problems at all. None. And that's the message here. A lesson for us all."

"I agree, Admiral," said Ryan. "He's certainly demonstrated how far you can go on sheer guts."

"And an amazing will to survive." Moorer turned to the briefing officer. "Colonel, I want to be kept right up to speed on this, advised of every development."

"Yes, sir."

Moorer leaned back in his chair and spoke softly, almost to himself. "The President himself is interested in the progress of this man."

Hambleton's head went under. He came up spitting and choking. He was getting so feeble he could not keep a firm grip on the slippery log. He put both arms around it to keep from sliding off. He looked at his watch. If it was still working it would soon be dawn, but he had twenty yards to go on this last hole.

Twenty yards. Didn't sound like much. But could he make them? It had taken three hours to shoot the seventeenth, and almost two hours of rest before he could even crawl back onto his log and start the eighteenth. This last hole had been the toughest of all. The river had turned east and broadened, reducing the speed of what little current there was. He had had to pull himself along the bank, grabbing overhanging brush to propel himself forward. It would have been a back-breaking chore for a man in good physical condition, let alone for one who was beginning to resemble a corpse.

Fifteen yards. That damned Birddog pilot had shown absolutely no sympathy. Had been no help whatsoever—egging him on, getting him mad. Buzzing him when he wouldn't talk to him on the radio, or when he was trying to sleep on the log. If he ever met him he'd hang, draw, and quarter him. Absolutely no respect for age or rank. Insubordinate little bastard.

Ten yards. Promising a clubhouse after the eighteenth hole! Come on! Who were they kidding? Did they actually think he was going to fall for that? Why were they suckering him along, giving him false hopes to cling to? Fighting to keep him alive—for what?

Five yards. OK. He could make five yards. Go all the way. Just to prove to that smart-assed FAC airplane driver that he could. When he finished the game and there was no clubhouse he was going to throw rocks at that buzzing son of a bitch.

He was startled by something in the river up ahead, coming straight at him. He squinted blurry eyes, trying to bring them into focus. Was it the Loch Ness monster? No. It was a snake. The biggest damned snake he had ever seen, coming at him, eyeball to eyeball. He slapped the water. The snake took off, zig-zagging across the river.

Damn good thing. That frigging reptile come any closer, he'd have bit his head off, skinned and eaten him.

He clicked off the four hundred and fifteenth yard—the distance of the eighteenth hole at Tucson National. Just up ahead was a small indenture in the river, with a sloping, muddy bank. Slipping, falling, floundering, he grunted the log up to the bank and gave it a last energy-sapping shove to secure it in the mud. Then he flopped down beside it. This was it.

Rescue or no rescue, he could go no farther. This was the end of his rope.

He looked around. No clubhouse. No line of golf carts. No pro shop. No bar. Just a line of thick brush that ran down to the muddy bank. He wiped a mud splat from his eye and fumbled for his radio. It took both hands to punch it on and get it to his mouth. "Birddog ... from Bat Twenty-one."

"Roger, Bat. How you doing?"

That cheery goddamn voice. He'd like to throttle it. "Have finished ... the last hole."

"Outstanding!"

"But...somebody moved the clubhouse."

"Just relax. Tote up your score. And keep your eyes open."

"Wilco ... Bat out." And he was out. Too weak to even crawl into the underbrush, he rolled over next to the log and, from sheer reflex, covered himself with mud as best he could, digging in like a salamander. Only his eyeballs moved.

Looking for God only knew what.

The biting of a mosquito on his cheek snapped Hambleton awake. Too tired to swat it, he simply shoved it off his face. Should he try and summon the strength to put on his mosquito netting? No. To hell with it. It hurt too damned much to move. The pain of his shoulder was a throbbing ache. He rolled over on his side to favor it. As he did so he saw something that chilled the very marrow in his bones. He blinked, hoping it was a dream. It was no dream. Oh, sweet Jesus, no! *No!* Not after all this. *Not after all this!*

He stared, bereft of hope, at the Vietnamese sampan coming around the bend of the river.

Silently it came, materializing in the dawn mist like some horrible apparition. In the prow of the boat was a Vietnamese, paddling slowly.

Hambleton went rigid. Should he try and make a break for it? Would his dead limbs respond even if he tried?

The sampan came closer. He could not think straight. He had to do something—at least crawl into the underbrush. Maybe he could make it ... but his extremities were no longer taking orders. Struck dumb with fear, he could only watch as the sampan slowly swung into the little cove and headed directly for his railroad tie.

Now it was too late even to call Birddog. The sampan gomers would hear. Why the hell hadn't he brought his gun? If he were doomed, he might at least go down fighting. Stealthily he reached for his knife, trying not to breathe. If he were spotted he would play dead, and when the Vietnamese came over to investigate, he would spring. Catch him unawares. If he could move.

The sampan nuzzled the bank right next to his tie. Hambleton mustered his last ounce of strength, readying to strike as soon as the Vietnamese disembarked.

But the Vietnamese seemed in no hurry to get out of the boat. He merely sat there quietly, his oar resting in his lap, the slow dripping of his paddle a metronome clicking off eons.

At first he thought it was a mirage created by his burning eyes trying to peer through clenched lids and muddy glasses. But then it happened again. The banana leaves stacked in the center of the boat moved. Then before his unbelieving eyes two of the large fronds parted and he found himself staring into a pair of eyes that were peering at him from under the leaves.

Hambleton blinked. *Not Oriental eyes—round eyes!* The roundest eyes he had ever seen!

"What's your dog's name?" queried a low voice.

Hambleton tried to speak, to squeeze words around his swollen tongue. He swallowed, then tried again. "P—Pierre."

"Congratulations, Colonel. You've just finished the eighteenth hole."

It took both the men in the sampan—the Vietnamese and the Marine Ranger—to roll Hambleton into the longboat and get him covered with the banana leaves. Then the sampan nosed back into the river, the sinewy shoulders of the diminutive Vietnamese Ranger in the prow bending to the oar.

As they headed downstream Hambleton looked out from under the leaves. Above them were two Sandys patrolling both sides of the river. Above the Sandys was a flight of Phantoms stitching vapor trails in the dawn sky.

The Ranger produced a canteen; he unscrewed the cap and handed it to Hambleton. "Nothing like a brisk eighteen holes to stir a man's thirst."

Hambleton thanked him with his eyes and took a long pull.

"Sorry it's not a cold Manhattan, but we'll take care of that shortly. Got some Jolly Greens waiting for us a couple clicks downstream."

Hambleton nodded and managed a tired grin. "Name's Hambleton," he said, foolishly, trying to extend his hand.

"I know," said the Marine. "I'm Lieutenant Morris. Call me Tom."

"Thanks, Tom."

"Anytime, Colonel."

Hambleton lay back. He couldn't convince himself it was true. He had been found. He was among friends. He was still far from safe, for the gauntlet of the enemy-held river still had to be run. But at least he was no longer alone.

With his pickup he had expected the Rangers to move out into the river and lay into those paddles. But they hadn't. They were going slowly along the bank, hugging the shoreline, taking advantage of the overhang. After an hour of almost smothering silence and snail-pace travel, the Vietnamese whispered, "We stop."

It was obvious the American Ranger had confidence in the small Vietnamese, for they stopped immediately. It had also soon become apparent the Vietnamese knew all the roads that led down to the river and where all the little villages were located. The sampan moved in tight against the bank, completely covered by overhang. The Vietnamese Ranger spread the foliage apart carefully and nodded downstream. "Look."

On the left bank, half a mile away and high up on a hill, were enemy soldiers. Hambleton now knew for sure that his transmissions had been monitored and triangulated by the enemy. A welcoming party was gathering to meet them. The Vietnamese Ranger turned to Morris. "Get on radio. Get help."

Morris did as instructed. He reached for his backpack radio, opened his map, and called the FAC. He gave Birddog his coordinates, then, "Black hats are going to try and head us off at the pass. Can you do something?"

"Roger," said Birddog. "We're riding shotgun. Pull in your neck."

They sat quietly, blending into the overhang, the stillness violated only by the dripping of sampan oars and the hum of insects. They could hear the voices of the soldiers as they came closer, crashing through the brush.

Hambleton peered nervously out of his camouflage. He could see the hill off to the left, and the small figures darting through the brush toward them. He sucked in his breath. With nothing else to do but keep a nervous eye on the approaching enemy, he turned on his radio low and listened to the chatter as Birddog talked to the unseen fighter pilots overhead.

Finally came the sight they had been waiting for. A white phosphorous flower blossomed precisely in the phalanx of the advancing soldiers. Then followed the words he knew would come. It was the steady, almost bored voice of Birddog. "Target's marked, gents. Here's your chance to be heroes. Applejack, bring in your flight first."

Down they came. The F-4's sundering the silence, their guns belching and their sonic booms sending visible shock waves undulating across the river. Two elements came in, pockmarking the earth around the phosphorous plume, reducing the surrounding woods to matchsticks.

For a full five minutes the devastation rained. Finally the last Phantom, having expended its ordnance, rocketed away to its base to be rearmed. When the final rumble from the enfilade had spent its echo against the hills, Morris took out a small pair of binoculars from his backpack. He swept the area with the glasses. Satisfied, he handed the glasses to the Vietnamese, who did likewise.

Morris looked down at Hambleton. "Those Zoomies are sure as hell noisy. Friends of yours?"

Hambleton nodded, smiling.

"A surly lot."

"Ain't it the truth. You should ... play poker with 'em sometime."

The Vietnamese said, "We go now."

The two men started paddling silently. They glided along, skirting the shore, the small Oriental in the prow turning his head from side to side, listening, sniffing the air. Downstream a ways he motioned toward the opposite bank, and they crossed the river, circumventing a small island and moving silently to the overhang on the west bank. For another half hour they skimmed along slowly until again the Vietnamese lifted his hand and dragged his paddle. "We stop." He pointed through the leaves and said, "Look."

There they were, a small detachment of soldiers on the east side, waiting quietly.

"Need help," said the Vietnamese.

Morris nodded, picked up his backpack radio, and began to transmit. There was no response. He could not raise Birddog. Nor, by switching channels, could he raise anyone else. His radio was dead. He tried everything short of kicking it, then looked questioningly at Hambleton. Hambleton handed his survival radio to the Ranger. "Try mine. Should work. Air Force equipment."

The Ranger took it and tried transmitting. Birddog responded immediately. Giving Hambleton an insouciant look, Morris again gave coordinates to Birddog. Then they sat back and waited.

Minutes later the Sandys came in. They each made several runs, and again all was quiet. The guide moved the big green leaves apart and peered out at the river bank ahead. His white teeth showed in a smile as he looked back and said, "We go again."

It was midmorning. For over three hours they had been on the river, gliding silently, seeking cover in the foliage, their bodies wet with sweat from a relentless sun that bored down through a cloudless sky. Where in hell was the fog when they needed it? Several times they came within range of sniper fire, the zing of bullets terminating in splashing thuds near the boat before they could maneuver away from the area. As the hours passed, dragging their heels, Hambleton began to wonder where they were taking him. He thought it was to be a short boat trip. He had assumed a helicopter would be waiting not far from where he had been picked up, but they kept moving on.

After carefully nosing around a large bend in the river, the guide once again whispered back, "We stop."

No one asked why. The eagle-eyed Vietnamese had proved himself right all the way on this journey, and there was bound to be a reason. There was a threat lurking in the green hills ahead. Hiding the boat as best they could, the Ranger peered through the leaves of a large banana plant. And then Hambleton and Morris saw it too—dead ahead. The barrel of a large gun lay some distance away. It was flanked by a group of soldiers, and was mounted in the turret of a tank. From Hambleton's vantage point the 76-mm looked huge, and so did the pillboxlike turret and the tracked, scowlike hull of the amphibious monster.

The Marine let out a low whistle, then checked in with Birddog, stating the problem. A Russian-made PT-76 reconnaissance tank would take a lot of discouraging. Birddog acknowledged, and again the escapees listened to the jargon as the FAC pilot organized the attack.

The covering planes came screaming down again, but it turned out to be nearly a twenty-minute job. The North Vietnamese had backed up their tank with antiaircraft machine guns spotted in the surrounding woods. It became a real contest before the tank was finally neutralized and the soldiers disappeared.

As the last Phantom made its pass, a transmission came over the radio that clutched Hambleton's heart with icy fingers. It was a simple, terse message from Birddog:

"Leatherneck, got a problem," came the cool voice. "Picked up a hit. Headin' for the barn. Will send an FAC replacement. Birddog out."

Hambleton snatched up the binoculars and searched the sky. And then he spotted the O-2 low on the horizon, hedgehopping over the hills. A stream of blue smoke was trailing the little plane as it disappeared over a distant rise.

"Dear God in heaven," muttered Hambleton, his eyes glued to the lingering veil of smoke, "get that pilot home safely."

"We go now," whispered the Vietnamese.

Another half hour passed as the boat made its way gingerly along the bank, giving a wide berth to the tank that was now nothing but a smoking hulk abandoned by its crew. Hambleton tried to take his mind off the crippled Birddog and address himself to the problems at hand, but it was impossible. He didn't even know the pilot's name. If Hambleton survived it would be because of some faraway detached voice whose owner he had never met. It was weird. A man had laid his life on the line for him many times, and he wouldn't even recognize him on the street. Unless he spoke. He would forever know that voice; the low voice that had cheered him, cajoled, badgered, nagged, and cursed him into hanging on—the voice that had been branded in his brain.

The sampan nosed into the shelter of a small cove. Another delay? Hambleton managed to prop himself up on his elbows and peer out of his concealment.

Something was moving! Were his bleary eyes fooling him? That tree. It looked like it was moving. By God, it *was* moving! And so was that bush beside it. And so was the next. Good Lord, the scenery was coming to life!

He felt a warm hand over his mouth. And then he looked up to see the Ranger smiling down at him. "Relax, Colonel," he said. "These Vietnamese wear white hats. Don't let the camouflage throw you."

The Vietnamese speaking in low, hurried voices came to the water's edge and waited. The Ranger assisted Hambleton out of the boat and scooped up his gear. "Come on, Colonel. We've got to make it to the top of that little hill. And fast."

The sound of ground fire echoed in the distance. Spurning helping hands, with an effort Hambleton tried to mount wobbling legs and join the men who were scrambling off into the brush. He staggered a few yards after them, and then his legs turned to Jell-O. He fell in a heap on the bank. He no sooner hit the ground than he was swooped up and thrown over the shoulders of a sinewy Vietnamese half his size. As if he were no heavier than a bag of rice, the Asian trotted with him through the undergrowth and did not stop until they had surmounted the small hill. At the top he was gently lowered to the ground.

A few yards away stood a cement blockhouse. Incongruous, squatting there in the jungle; it could have been transplanted from the Normandy beachhead or the Maginot Line. Obviously it was a legacy from the days of the French in Southeast Asia, the days before they had met their Waterloo at Dien Bien Phu.

He was helped inside the cement bastion and stretched out on a litter. Someone covered him with a blanket to ward off the musty chill, while someone else took off his heavy, waterlogged shoes and socks. Another Samaritan began massaging the numbed chunks of lead his feet had become, kneading them back to life by restarting circulation.

Outside it sounded like hell was erupting. The chatter of stuttering machine guns mixed with sporadic rifle fire and the resounding thump of mortars that appeared to be directed at the blockhouse. Heavier stuff soon started chiming in as well, ricocheting shrapnel fragments off the three-foot-thick walls of the concrete fort.

Oblivious of the pandemonium going on outside, tender hands ministered to Hambleton's needs, giving him water to drink, a small bottle of wine which he sampled. And then, glory of glories, someone parted his lips with the butt of a cigarette. Goddamn! He took a big drag, inhaling deeply, and promptly went into a coughing spasm. His eyes watered as he fought to get his breath. Damn, it tasted good!

Lieutenant Morris came in and sat down beside his litter. "We're going to need more help, Colonel. Bastards are really pissed. They're trying to surround us."

"I thought we were supposed to be out of the firefight zone?"

"You know it and I know it. But somebody forgot to clue in the Commies. Damn, they go down hard. They must want you awful bad."

Feeling giddy from the swallow of wine and the unaccustomed nicotine, Hambleton managed a half grin. "Now you know what it's like ... to have your picture on the post office wall."

Morris looked at him oddly. "Have to borrow your radio again. Kills my heart to do it, but we'll have to ask the Air Force for more help."

"They don't mind. They're on our side."

Morris ducked out the door to make his radio call.

For an hour the ground rocked with the reverberations of Air Force ordnance striking close—at times too damned close, all but knocking Hambleton out of his litter. During the bombardment the Vietnamese never left his side and kept wiping his face with wet rags.

At long last it ended, and all was still.

Morris came into the blockhouse, groping his way through the cement dust that filled the clammy air inside the small building. "Well, Colonel, the zoomies have pretty well clobbered the trouble spots. Time to get it in gear and get you out of here."

"Let's go," said Hambleton, trying to raise himself up from his litter.

"Just stay put. We'll take care of you."

Hambleton couldn't argue or resist. He lay back on the litter as instructed. And then he heard a noise that made him frown. Was he mistaken, or was that the sound of metal treads clanking outside? The natives heard it too, and were talking excitedly. He looked questioningly at the lieutenant.

"It's all right, Colonel," said Morris. "It's ours. Your taxi."

Before he knew what was happening, Hambleton found himself whisked out of the blockhouse on his litter and put into the personnel carrier. His rescuers clambered up on the top, clinging there to keep an alert lookout for the enemy. Then the machine started off down the hill at top speed, those riding shotgun opening up with bursts from time to time from their M-16 rifles.

Growling along in the bowels of the steaming machine which was making roads where there were no roads, each jolt was agony, each bump sent stabs of pain that penetrated his numbed senses. Hambleton lost track of time. He had surrendered the responsibility of keeping track of such things to someone else. The load had been removed from his shoulders and draped over those of his rescuers. He hardly realized that well over an hour had passed when the carrier finally ground to a halt.

Again he found himself lifted on the litter, and then he was out of the carrier and on the ground, the warm breeze feeling good on his sweating body. And then he looked around, and his eyes fell on the most beautiful sight he had ever seen.

Parked in a small clearing was a Jolly Green!

Soon he was bouncing over the ground at breakneck speed on

his stretcher, and then he was in the chopper and a corpsman was saying let's get the hell out of here, and then the rotor blades were turning.

The chopper blades screwed through the humid air, and even as Hambleton felt the pull of gravity on his innards, he was being stripped and examined. Efficient fingers flew over his body; he felt like a race car as paramedics hovered over him like mechanics in a pit stop. They put a needle in his arm and started intravenous feeding. They seemed to stick needles everywhere. One medic looked at his index finger and Hambleton winced as the corpsman shook his head. They worked on his left arm and he heard the word fracture. Disinfectant was applied to his wounds, medical cream was rubbed on his feet to help the circulation. He was being made as comfortable as possible for the flight to the field hospital.

On gaining a safe altitude and swinging out over friendly territory, the chopper pilot turned around and shouted back to his passenger. "Welcome to the clubhouse, Colonel."

Hambleton made a circle of his thumb and forefinger, and lifted it to the pilot.

The Thirteenth Day

Gwen Hambleton was having one of her nightmares when the shrill jangle of the telephone brought her springing up from her pillow. She sat for a moment in the dim glow of the night-light, trying to compose herself. The phone rang again. She reached over to the bed lamp, switched it on, and glanced at the clock. Three-twenty in the morning.

She guessed it had to be news, either good or bad. The casualty center had promised to call with word of any development no matter the hour. A chill ran down her backbone.

She lifted the phone from its cradle on the third ring, held it for several seconds, then put the receiver to her ear.

"Gwen Hambleton speaking."

"This is Sergeant Smith from the Casualty Division of the Air Force Military Personnel Center. I'm sorry to be calling you at this late hour. But I'm sure you'll understand. It's about your husband, Colonel Hambleton. We've just received a message from the Three Eighty-eighth Tactical Fighter Wing. Your husband has been rescued and returned to military control."

Gwen felt the blood gushing to her head. The phone slipped from her grasp. "Oh, dear God!"

"Mrs. Hambleton? Are you all right?"

She picked up the phone. "Yes...yes, Sergeant, I'm all right. I'm quite all right."

"Look, Mrs. Hambleton, good news can sometimes be just as much of a shock as bad. If you like I'll have someone dispatched from the base hospital at Davis—"

"Thank you, no, Sergeant. I'm quite all right now. It took a moment for it to sink in. But I've never been quite so all right in my entire life. Are there any other details?"

"The initial report is pretty fragmentary, but I can tell you this. Your husband has been returned to Da Nang Air Base in South Vietnam. He was not seriously injured. But he's suffering from exhaustion and dehydration."

"Then he's going to be OK."

"I'd say so, ma'am. If you wish, you can address mail to him at the Ninety-eighth Medical Evacuation Hospital, APO San Francisco, 96337. But you don't need to write that down now unless you want to. A confirming telegram will be dispatched to you within the hour."

"I'm too excited right now, Sergeant. The telegram will be fine."

"Very good. You have our number here at the casualty center. Please let us know if there is any way we may be of assistance. Day or night."

"That's very kind."

"Our pleasure. And congratulations on the safe return of your husband."

"Thank you, Sergeant. Thank you very, *very* much."

She cradled the phone, then let the dam break. She gave full vent to her twelve-day lifetime of worries, fears, anxieties, and a gnawing helplessness—letting them dissolve unchecked into handfuls of Kleenex.

When she had cried herself out, she went and washed her face, combed her hair, and put on the new dressing gown she had bought for her trip to Bangkok. Then she made a circuit through the house, turning on every light in the place. A puzzled Pierre joined her, his drowsiness quickly transformed into joy as he became infected with her high spirits. She turned on the stereo, then dropped down onto the sofa.

Pierre jumped beside her, his tail wagging in overdrive.

"Poppa's coming home, Pierre," she said, hugging the dog. "Poppa's coming home."

On the flight line of the Korat Royal Thai Air Force Base, Captain Clark was saying good-bye to his roommate, Campbell, before boarding the plane for Vietnam. From there he was to catch his flight to the States.

"Thanks for everything, Jake. It's been a fun war."

"Hasn't it?" Campbell shook the pilot's hand. "But you're making a big mistake not sticking around for your farewell party. This is the eighth I've thrown for you. Sure you wouldn't like to make at least one?"

"Some other time."

"You should see the new Red Cross gal that just checked in. Absolutely gorgeous! She's got—"

"I know. I saw her. Legs like a Green Bay Packer."

"Oh, you saw her. Well, over here you can't be too picky."

"That's why I'm leaving."

"Okay, coward," Campbell looked into the face of his friend. "Rumor has it you're going to get some kind of a medal."

"A medal? Oh, joy. What the hell for?"

"Walker likes the way you land shot-up airplanes. The guy's crazy."

"I don't know about that. You notice I had the foresight to land in friendly territory."

"Yeah, but in a river?"

"Listen. Any landing you can walk away from is..."

"I know." There was an awkward silence, then, "Well. Here comes your plane. Hate long good-byes. Just promise me one thing, will you, roomie?"

"Name it."

"Promise you won't write. I hate to answer letters."

"It's a promise."

"So long, stud." The little finance officer turned on his heel. "It's sure as hell been..."

"It sure as hell has, Jake. Hang loose."

Clark picked up his flight bag and headed for the old C-47 that was to take him to Saigon. He threw his bag on board, and was just about to follow it when he felt a tap on his shoulder. He turned. It was Frank Ott.

"Glad I caught you, Clark. Wanted to say good-bye."

"I'm glad you did, Colonel."

"Sorry I missed you before. I was on the horn trying to get through to Hambleton."

"No kidding. Any luck?"

Ott nodded. "I finally got through. He's at the hospital in Da Nang, and all in one piece."

"How's he doing?"

"Complaining about some big cow of a nurse that keeps trying to give him an enema. Claims that's the last thing in the world he needs."

Clark grinned. "There's no understanding medics. They're worse than fighter pilots."

"So you're bugging out. Leaving us with our little war."

"Afraid so. I just stuck around for the golf game."

"It was some game."

"Helluva game. Hope your war comes out the same way."

"This war!" Ott snorted. "Reminds me of a little gem Piccard dug up: This damn war is a conflict which does not determine who is right—but who is left. Sure as hell nails this one."

"Good point. Next war we'll let the politicians fight it."

"Amen." Ott held out his hand. "Well, it looks like the jocks are about ready to crank up this bucket of bolts. Good-bye, Clark. And good luck."

"Good-bye, Colonel. Same to you. Thanks for coming."

As Clark turned to start up the steps, Ott stopped him again. "Oh, one thing. When I talked to Hambleton, just before he hung up he asked if I knew your name."

"Did you tell him?"

"I did. It would be rather amusing if you two met up some day."

"That it would. Who knows?"

"So long, Clark."

"Good-bye, Colonel."

As the crew chief bolted the door, Clark swung a bucket seat down from the side of the aircraft and strapped himself in. The airplane gave a lurch and started to taxi as he hunched forward to look out of the window.

His mind a million light-years away, he watched the blue taxi lights float by in the still Thai night.

Hambleton glared at the big nurse bending over him. "No way, nurse. No way."

"Now, Colonel, let's not be obstinate. You're not the first, and you'll not be the last patient to use a bedpan."

"I hate to pull rank, Major, but..."

"There is no rank in this ward, Colonel. Now let's not get waspish."

"Let's get waspish. I didn't escape from the gomers to come here and..."

"Colonel Hambleton?"

Hambleton turned to look at the source of the welcome interruption. A young medical corpsman was standing in the doorway. He was holding a phone with an extension line that disappeared into the hall. "Yes?" said Hambleton.

"Sir, this is a bit unusual, but you have a long-distance phone call. Can you take it?"

Hambleton looked defiantly at the nurse. "Of course."

"It's the Pentagon," said the corpsman. He held the phone as if it were about to bite him.

"I'll take it."

"The doctor thought it was a gag at first," said the corpsman, bringing the phone over to Hambleton's bed. "But it's not." He handed the receiver to Hambleton. "It's an Admiral Moorer."

Hambleton took the receiver. Christ! The Chairman of the Joint Chiefs of Staff!

He started to speak, but nothing came. He swallowed and tried again. "This is Colonel Hambleton."

The voice on the other end was low. "Admiral Moorer, Colonel. How are you?"

"Fine, sir. Thank you."

"Welcome back. Understand you've been getting in a little golf."

"Been keeping my hand in. Yes, sir."

"Are they taking good care of you there at the hospital?"

Hambleton shot a meaningful look at the nurse. "No problems, sir."

"If you need anything, just let me know. I just wanted to call personally and welcome you back. On behalf of General Ryan and the other services, we're mighty glad you're with us again. Congratulations, it was one hell of a job."

"Thank you, sir. But the credit doesn't go to me. There were a lot of people who were in on it."

"I know. It was a fine team effort. It's good to know that we can all pull together once in a while and get something constructive out of the effort."

"Thank you, sir, for calling. I appreciate it very much. Believe me."

"My pleasure. Oh, just one more thing. I think you might

enjoy knowing that the officers here in the Pentagon have really turned into a bunch of sporting types."

"Oh?"

"They're all working on their golf game."

Hambleton chuckled.

"Best wishes, Hambleton, for a speedy recovery. We're looking forward to seeing you in Washington. Good-bye."

"Good-bye, sir."

When the corpsman disappeared with the phone, Hambleton lay back on his pillow and studied the ceiling. The phone call had sort of made it all official. He was alive. He had made it, and he was going to see Gwen and Pierre and his old friends. He was going to play golf and drink Manhattans and he was going to have to buy drinks for a hell of a lot of people. In the last two weeks he had learned a lot about other people.

But above all, he had learned about himself. More than he had ever dreamed of knowing. Maybe more than he wanted to know; maybe more than any man should ever know about himself. He had looked long and hard into that full-length mirror of adverse circumstance. It had reflected his strengths—and his weaknesses— revelations made to few men. He had not liked some of the things he had seen. But, all things considered, he could live with those reflections.

He sighed. It had been an experience. It had been one hell of an experience.

His musings were suddenly interrupted by the sound of a voice coming from the hall. There was something oddly familiar about it, and then as it got closer he propped himself up on his elbows, thunderstruck.

"Birddog calling Bat Twenty-one," came the words from the hallway. "Do you read Birddog?"

"For God's sake!" stammered Hambleton. "Bat Twenty-one here. Come in, Birddog."

And then Captain Clark was framed in the doorway, dressed in his suntans and carrying an incongruous vase of flowers. He stood for a moment, awkwardly, staring at the man in the bed.

Hambleton returned an astonished, wide-eyed stare, then blurted, "Well, I'm a son of...you're *black!*"

Clark approached the foot of the bed. He looked down at his hands, smiled, and said, "Well, whaddaya know. So I am."

Hambleton shook his head, trying to marshal his thoughts. "I've spent hours picturing you in my mind. And it never once dawned on me that you might be black."

"You got something against night fighters?" asked Clark, grinning.

Hambleton laughed. "From now on I'm painting all my guardian angels black. "Lord, let me shake your hand." Hambleton took the proffered hand in his own and squeezed it with all the strength he could muster. "I heard you landed in the river."

"When your airplane's on fire, can you think of a better way to put it out?"

Hambleton shook his head, grinning. "You are something else, Birddog."

"Might say the same about you, Bat."

They locked eyes, saying nothing, silence speaking volumes. Presently the nurse materialized from the background. "I hate to break up this tender scene," she said, "but Captain, you'll have to go."

Clark turned to the nurse. "All right, Major." He went to the nightstand, put down the vase of flowers. As he did, he leaned down to whisper into Hambleton's ear. "If you let the nurse change the water in this vase, a quart of Manhattans goes down the drain."

Hambleton looked at the smiling pilot. Then he said softly, "You're one hell of a guardian angel, Birddog."

"See ya around, Bat Twenty-one."

"Roger, Birddog. See ya around."

Clark popped a half-assed salute and went out the door.

Hambleton stared at the empty doorway, listening to the staccato of Clark's retreating boots, his face a study of emotion. He stayed transfixed until the footsteps faded to a lingering echo.

A sound caused him to turn his head. The nurse was advancing on him, carrying something wrapped in a towel. As she handed him the bedpan, and as he reached out for it, he detected the flash of victory shining in her face. But then it faded as smiling, he placed the bedpan on the nightstand. He struggled to a sitting position and swung his feet to the floor.

Before she even had a chance to protest, he took her hand, clinching the victory.

"Come, my dear," he said, picking up his vase of flowers. "You may escort me to the bathroom."

Author's Afterword

Readers may have noted that the subtitle of this book reads "Based on the true story of Lieutenant Colonel Iceal E. Hambleton, USAF." Why "based on"? Is it Hambleton's story or isn't it? The answer is yes, in spirit and in most essential details it *is* the story of Hambleton's experience, just as it happened; but it is also true that some changes have been made. The purpose of this Afterword is to set the record straight—to explain what the changes are, why I made them, and, along the way, to give credit to some brave men whose names do not appear in the text.

When I first sat down to write the story of the twelve-day ordeal of my friend Gene Hambleton, I had every intention of adhering scrupulously to the facts. If I had any reservation at all about this it was only that the facts themselves sounded so much like fiction that the reader might not believe them. But as the writing progressed I began to encounter more pressing difficulties. The first and most serious of these was that certain parts of the story which seemed important to me were still classified—particularly certain aspects of Air Force escape and evasion techniques. Further, I was requested to protect the identity of certain individuals. Since I felt I could neither gloss over nor ignore these elements in the narrative, I would necessarily have to replace them with some fictions approximate to the truth. Thus, almost from the beginning, my original intention of sticking strictly to the facts had to go by the boards.

There was another difficulty as well. Although it had nothing to do with the facts, it was to me, as a writer, particularly worrisome. It was that, taken all in all, the actual rescue effort made on

Hambleton's behalf was so complex, involved so many people, made use of such complex logistics and (in some cases) such exotic technology, that there was a very real danger that the central narrative of Hambleton's ordeal might be swamped in peripheral detail. In view of this I began to wonder if truth might not be better served if some of this detail could be both simplified and introduced in such a way that the reader would not be overwhelmed by it.

After some soul-searching, I finally decided to employ a narrative device that would solve a great many of the complications worrying me. This was to interpolate into the story a fictional character who would perform the roles actually played by a rather populous cast of real people operating at different times and from separate geographical locations. That character is Captain Dennis Clark, the dedicated FAC pilot whose (also fictitious) call sign is Birddog. Originally I wanted him to stand for several teams of FAC pilots operating out of both Da Nang Air Base in South Vietnam and Nakhon Phanom Air Base in Thailand during the period of the Bat-21 rescue operation; but in time I began to see him as representative of all the heroic, unsung FAC pilots who—throughout the long, bitter struggle in Vietnam—daily risked their lives for their service and their country.

Once Dennis Clark stepped onto the scene, certain other changes had to be made. Since several real people had now been omitted from the story, the sequence of a few events had to be altered to account for their subtraction from the narrative. Thus, while the central story of Hambleton's experience remained intact, the chain of events relating to the rescue effort could no longer be exact.

Gene Hambleton has been kind enough to agree that the liberties I have taken in the telling of his story were acceptable and realistic. I hope you will too, for at no point have I knowingly violated the overall sequence and structure of the facts in this case, departed from the daily realities of Air Force operations at this period in the Vietnam conflict, or resorted to any anachronisms or technical impossibilities. My sole objective throughout has been to make this extraordinary story as coherent, immediate and accessible for the reader as possible.

It is only fair to try and give you a summary of some of the salient events in the sequence in which they actually occurred, along with the names of some of the more prominent members of the real cast of characters who were involved. This brief recap hardly does justice to what was, in fact, the largest mission to rescue a downed airman in U.S. Air Force history. I hope, however, it is sufficient to convey some idea of the sequence and complexity of the actual events.

When Hambleton ejected from his stricken EB-66, the orbiting FAC pilot he contacted while still descending in his parachute was Captain Jimmie D. Kempton, piloting an OV-10 out of Da Nang AB. After the A-IEs had sanitized the area surrounding Hambleton, Kempton tried to call in a rescue force of two UH-IB Cobra helicopter gunships and two UH-IH passenger-carrying Slick helicopters. While approaching the area where Hambleton was located, enemy antiaircraft fire destroyed one UH-IH and so damaged a Cobra that the force was obliged to retire.

Throughout the night Da Nang FACs (call signs Covey or Bilk) and Nakhon Phantom FACs (call sign Nail) maintained constant patrol over Hambleton. In the morning, two Nail FACs, one crewed by Captains Rock O. Smith and Richard M. Atchison, took up station over the downed navigator, calling in more protective air strikes during the day.

The following day another FAC, Nail 38, crewed by Captains William Henderson and Mark Clark, relieved Smith and Atchison. Almost immediately upon arrival this aircraft was hit and destroyed by a SAM-2. Both crewmen succeeded in bailing out. Henderson was taken prisoner, but Clark evaded capture and—like Hambleton—hid in the jungle, awaiting rescue.

Other Da Nang and Nakhon Phantom FACs immediately replaced Nail-38, keeping station over Hambleton and Clark and calling in successive air strikes during the next several days. It was, in fact, a Covey FAC who acted as controller for the B-52 raid.

As described in the text, on April 6 an HH-53 helicopter, Jolly-62, escorted by two A-1Es, attempted to rescue both downed airmen, but was shot down by antiaircraft fire in the attempt.

Although Hambleton, the FAC, and the Sandys all had tried to warn Jolly-62 not to make a right turn over a village known to contain antiaircraft emplacements, the helicopter pilot never responded. It has been surmised that he was holding down his radio's transmit button at the time, thus preventing his receiving the warning messages.

Thereafter, while senior Air Force officers and Pentagon officials debated what to do next, successive teams of FACs, controlling many more protective air-to-ground strikes, continued to watch over the downed airmen.

Hambleton's eventual rescue occurred essentially as described in the text. Clark, being nearer to the Mieu Giang River, swam and floated downstream to meet the Marine/ARVN rescue team first. It took Hambleton, who had a longer distance to go and much more dangerous terrain to cross, four days to reach the rendezvous point. This he finally did on April 14.

Colonel Hambleton's rescue did not end his misfortunes. In addition to being blasted out of bed by a Communist rocket attack on the hospital in Da Nang, he was to suffer yet another trial. Airlifted to Clark Air Force Base in the Philippines, he arrived there the night one of the severest recorded earthquakes rocked the Islands and nearly destroyed the base hospital. Again, he emerged unscathed.

For his heroic efforts, ignoring personal safety in guiding fighters and bombers to key targets from his grandstand seat in the combat zone, Hambleton was awarded the Silver Star, Distinguished Flying Cross, Air Medal, and the Purple Heart. He has been released from the Air Force on a disability discharge, because of residual injuries suffered when he ejected from his aircraft.

He now lives with his wife, Gwen, in Tucson, Arizona.

Not far from a golf course.

William C. Anderson
California, 1980